SHAKESPEARE

KING LEAR
IN EVERYDAY
ENGLISH

COLES EDITORIAL BOARD

Bound to stay open

Publisher's Note

Otabind (Ota-bind). This book has been bound
using the patented Otabind process. You can
open this book at any page, gently run your
finger down the spine, and the pages will lie flat.

ABOUT COLES NOTES

COLES NOTES have been an indispensible aid to students on five continents since 1948.

COLES NOTES are available for a wide range of individual literary works. Clear, concise explanations and insights are provided along with interesting interpretations and evaluations.

Proper use of COLES NOTES will allow the student to pay greater attention to lectures and spend less time taking notes. This will result in a broader understanding of the work being studied and will free the student for increased participation in discussions.

COLES NOTES are an invaluable aid for review and exam preparation as well as an invitation to explore different interpretive paths.

COLES NOTES are written by experts in their fields. It should be noted that any literary judgement expressed herein is just that – the judgement of one school of thought. Interpretations that diverge from, or totally disagree with any criticism may be equally valid.

COLES NOTES are designed to supplement the text and are not intended as a substitute for reading the text itself. Use of the NOTES will serve not only to clarify the work being studied, but should enhance the readers enjoyment of the topic.

ISBN 0-7740-3735-0

© COPYRIGHT 1999 AND PUBLISHED BY
COLES PUBLISHING COMPANY
TORONTO - CANADA
PRINTED IN CANADA

Manufactured by Webcom Limited
Cover finish: Webcom's Exclusive **DURACOAT**

CHARACTERS IN THE PLAY

Lear: King of Britain.
King of France
Duke of Burgundy
Duke of Cornwall
Duke of Albany
Earl of Kent
Earl of Gloucester
Edgar: Gloucester's son.
Edmund: Bastard son of Gloucester.
Curan: A courtier.
Old Man: Gloucester's tenant.
Doctor
Lear's Fool
Oswald: Steward to Goneril.
A Captain under Edmund's command.
Gentlemen
A Herald
Servants of Cornwall.
Goneril
Regan } Lear's daughters.
Cordelia
Knights attending on Lear, Officers,
Messengers, Soldiers and Attendants.

[Setting: Ancient Britain.]

1

ACT I • SCENE 1

[King Lear's palace.]
[Enter Kent, Gloucester and Edmund.]

Kent: I always imagined that the king had a greater liking for the Duke of Albany than for the Duke of Cornwall.

Gloucester: That was our opinion also but he has shown preference for neither of them in sharing his realm between them. The parts are so evenly balanced that the most careful scrutiny could not find anything in the one to make it preferable to the other.

Kent: This is your son, is it not, sir?

Gloucester: I have had the responsibility of bringing him up and have so often been ashamed to admit the relationship that, now, I am hardened to it. But I love him as much as my lawful heir, who is a year or so older than this boy and, though the lad came unbidden, I keep him for his mother's sake. Do you know, my boy, who this nobleman is?

Edmund: I do not, sir.

Gloucester: It is the Earl of Kent. Do not forget that he is a worthy friend of mine.

Edmund: I am at your service, sir.

Kent: I hope we shall become better acquainted and I think I shall like you well.

Edmund: I shall try to deserve your respect, sir.

Gloucester: He has been abroad for several years, and I mean to send him away again. See, here comes the king!

[Enter sennet, bearing a coronet, King Lear, Cornwall, Albany, Goneril, Regan, Cordelia and attendants.]

Lear: My Lord of Gloucester, wait upon the princes of France and Burgundy.

Gloucester: Yes, your majesty.

[Exeunt Gloucester and Edmund.]

Lear: While we await their arrival, I will explain my further intentions with regard to the kingdom. Let me have the map before me. I announce to all present that I have divided my realm into three sections, and have fully resolved that I will henceforth be done with the burdens and responsibilities of state. I will leave them to be borne by younger shoulders than mine, while I, freed from such heavy cares, creep quietly towards the grave. My son, the Duke of Cornwall and you also of Albany, both equally dear to me, you must know that I have made up my mind to settle and announce at this present time the different dowry each of my daughters is to receive, so that there may be no danger of disputes in the future.

The decision will also interest the two noble princes who have made so lengthy a stay here in Britain, as suitors for the hand of my youngest daughter, Cordelia. They have remained here so long, hoping to obtain her affection, and now desire their answer. And now, my children, since I intend to lay aside my power and my wealth, as well as my responsibilities, I should like to know which of you feels the greatest affection for me, in order that I may reward that one, whose loving disposition deserves it, with the largest portion. My eldest daughter, Goneril, answer first.

Goneril: My king, the weightiest words are powerless to express my affection for you. I prize you more highly than freedom, or liberty of motion, or the power to look upon outward things. I hold you dearer than the most valuable thing on earth, no matter how costly. I love you as dearly as life itself, with all that makes life worth having. My love is as great as any child ever gave to its parent, or parent could receive from a child. It defies description and confounds all words. As much as this, and yet more, is the measure of my love for you.

Cordelia: *[Aside.]* What, then, can I do? I must be content to love in silence for, after this, words will be useless.

Lear: On you, Goneril, I bestow all this great tract of country between these boundaries, a land of fair meadows, well-watered plains and extensive forests. This shall be the inheritance of you and your heirs forever.

My well-loved Regan, married to the Duke of Cornwall, what say you?

Regan: You may esteem my love at exactly the same value as that of my sister. I am made of the same material as she is, and my love is as great. My inmost soul responds to her words, and she gives a voice to my very feelings, with this exception only: she does not go so far as I, for I vow that I can take pleasure in nothing else whatever, not in the most exquisite of delights, but only in your majesty's love. That is the only thing that gives me happiness.

Cordelia: *[Aside.]* Alas for me, then! Yet, I need not pity myself, since I have still a great wealth of affection, greater than any wealth of words.

Lear: I give to you, Regan, and to your heirs, in perpetual possession, this large portion of my realm, a portion as extensive, as beautiful and as valuable as that bestowed on your sister. To you now I turn, my loved one, my dear delight, whom I love no less than your sisters, though I leave your portion till the last. Cordelia, for whose affection the lords of those rich lands of France and Burgundy are rivals to each other, what vows of dutiful affection can you make, so that I may reward them with a greater wealth than the others have received? Let me hear you.

Cordelia: None, sire.

Lear: None!

Cordelia: No, my lord.

Lear: None of my bounty then can reward it. Answer me once more.

Cordelia: Alas! I am so unfortunate as to be unable to show my feelings in words. My affection for you, sire, is such as my duty implies, neither greater nor smaller.

Lear: Indeed, Cordelia! Try to improve your words somewhat, or your fortunes will certainly suffer.

Cordelia: My honored sire, I owe to you my life and my maintenance, and you have given me love besides. In return, I gladly give to you my affection, my obedience and my deepest reverence, as it is fitting I should do. If my sisters, as they profess, have given you all their affection, why have they married? If ever I marry, the man to whom I pledge myself will certainly receive at least half of my affection and respect and half the duty that I owe to those I love. If I were unable to bestow any of my love on any other man besides my father, as Regan and Goneril profess, I should not wed at all.

Lear: And does this express your true feelings?

Cordelia: Yes, your majesty.

Lear: Is it possible that one so youthful should be so cold?

Cordelia: It is possible to be youthful and still be honest.

Lear: Agreed. Then your honesty may be your portion, for I vow, by the holy rays of the life-giving sun, by the hidden rites of the dark goddess, Hecate, and by the mysterious planetary influences which rule life and death, that never from this moment will I acknowledge you as child of mine or claim a share in your blood and being, but look upon you, now and henceforth, as an utter stranger and outcast from my love. From this time, my heart will feel as kindly toward the most cruel of savage tribes or even toward the monster who devours his own children, as toward you, who were once my child.

Kent: My noble king . . .

Lear: Silence, my lord! Beware of interfering between a king and the object of his anger. Cordelia was dearer to me than any other, and I would have staked my all that I should peacefully end my days under her loving care. Away! Let me see you no more! As I hope to rest in the tomb, I here withdraw every spark of affection from such a daughter. Summon the two princes who desire her love. Well, who will obey? You, Duke of Albany and you of Cornwall, absorb Cordelia's portion into those of Regan and Goneril, your wives. Let Cordelia subsist on pride, which she thinks is honesty.

I here appoint you joint rulers of this realm and bestow upon you all the might and majesty, the privileges and splendor that belong to royalty. I reserve 100 knights as my own train and shall dwell with each of you in turn, to be maintained by you alternately for the space of a month. To me still belongs the style and title of king, but the power and authority, the wealth and the administration of the kingdom, I leave, my dear sons, in your hands. In proof of this, I herewith hand you my crown to be shared between you.

[Giving the crown.]

Kent: My lord and master, to whom I have always paid reverence as my sovereign, to whom I have yielded the obedience due from a servant, together with the affection of a son, and for whom I have petitioned heaven . . .

Lear: The arrow of my wrath is about to fly from the string. If you value your safety, avoid its path.

Kent: No, let it be released on me, though its point should pierce my bosom. When my king is insane, let me be stubborn. Consider what you do, sir, and do not think that a truly dutiful subject will be afraid to speak plainly when he sees flatterers exalted and majesty deceived by their false

5

words. Your truest friends are compelled, in honor, to speak plainly when your royal self descends to such foolish and unwise acts.

Retract the unjust sentence you have pronounced. Take careful thought and restrain yourself from committing such reckless acts. I will answer for my opinion with my life and say that young Cordelia's affection for you is fully as great as her sisters'. Vessels which give forth no sound are not the empty ones, nor is a heart void of affection, though its words are quiet and few.

Lear: If you value your life, be silent!

Kent: I never looked upon my life as anything but the humblest of your majesty's possessions, only to be used in your defence, nor am I afraid to have it taken from me, if thereby I may benefit my king.

Lear: Begone from my presence!

Kent: May your eyes be opened, so that you may see that I am one of your truest friends.

Lear: By the god of light!

Kent: Even by the god of light, your majesty, you summon your deities uselessly.

Lear: Slave! Villain!

[Laying his hand on his sword.]

Albany:
Cornwall: } Stop!

Kent: Yes, stop thy hand. Your action, my lord, is as foolish as that of the man who slays the one who would cure him and encourages the sickness from which he suffers. You severely punish the one whose truthful words are for your benefit and reward the flatterers whose vows make hers seem cold. Again, I say, retract your unjust sentence, or I will cry out against it as long as my tongue can utter a sound.

Lear: Listen to me, traitorous knight! By your vows of fidelity, attend my words! You have presumed to interfere when I have delivered judgment and seek to prevent the carrying out of the sentence I have pronounced. You have also urged me to break my word and alter my decision, which I have never yet done. Neither of these offences can I endure, either as a man or as a king. Therefore, now that my authority is defended and clearly understood, hear the result of your presumption. You will be allowed five days to make the necessary preparations and, on the day following, you must take your unwelcome self out of this country. If you should be discovered anywhere within my realm in ten days' time, your life will be instantly forfeited. Begone and, by the gods, I will retract not a word of this sentence!

Kent: Adieu, your majesty. Since this is your disposition, I should be as much a stranger at your court as though I were in exile. I will go and find true freedom elsewhere.

[To Cordelia.] May heaven protect and sustain you, sweet girl, who have a mind which thinks rightly and courage to speak truly.

[To Regan and Goneril.] And may your actions justify the boastful speeches you have uttered and the results prove that you meant all your words. Here, my lords, I take my farewell of you all and go to begin life again in a foreign land.

[Exit.]
[Flourish. Re-enter Gloucester, with France, Burgundy and attendants.]

Gloucester: My lord, the princes are here.

Lear: I will speak first to you, most noble Burgundy, who desires as does also the King of France, to gain my daughter's hand in marriage. I would ask what is the smallest dowry that you will accept for my daughter and without which you would cease to be a suitor for her hand.

Burgundy: Most noble king, I ask for nothing beyond what you have already promised and I feel sure your highness would not offer anything less.

Lear: Worthy duke, when I thought highly of my daughter, I placed her value high. Now, I think it much less than before. My lord, you see her before you. If you see anything there in that small frame which pleases you — or even her whole body, with the addition of her father's anger, but no other gift — then take her. There she stands for your acceptance on those terms.

Burgundy: I do not know what to say.

Lear: Do you take her, together with her faults and short-comings, friendless and having but recently incurred her father's displeasure, with no gift but a father's scorn and

7

with no home, having been cast off by him? Under these conditions, do you still seek her hand or not?

Burgundy: Your majesty must forgive me. It is not possible to make a choice under such circumstances.

Lear: It is better, then, that you should renounce her, my lord, for I swear by my Maker that she will possess no more than I have told you.

[To France.] And to you I say, mighty prince, that I will not be guilty of an act that would give you so little cause to love me as the arranging of a marriage with one who has incurred my hatred. So let me beg you to turn your regard in another direction and do not stoop to bestow your love on a miserable creature such as this, whom humanity must blush to own.

France: This seems a marvellous thing, that the maiden who, up till this moment, was your greatest delight, the constant theme of your praises, the solace of your advancing years and your best beloved, should suddenly appear to have committed some fault so terrible that it has caused her to lose so many degrees of your affection. The love that you formerly professed for her must surely have fallen greatly into decay, or else her misdeeds must be most atrocious, and that I will never credit. It is a belief that nothing short of a miracle could ever make me entertain.

Cordelia: I pray you, my lord, because I am unskilful in the use of words and cannot utter smooth phrases and deceitful flatteries (for I can perform my intentions much more readily than talk about them), let it be known that I have not lost your affection on account of any crime or tendency to vice or dishonorable action, but solely for the lack of something I am better without — an eye that covets all it sees and a tongue ready to utter words which I am glad to be unable to utter, though that inability has cost me a father's love.

Lear: I would rather never have had a daughter, Cordelia, than, having her, find that she so deserves my anger.

France: Is this all her fault — a hesitating speech and slowness of disposition, which finds itself unable often to give words to its thoughts and feelings? What is your real opinion of this maid, my lord duke? True affection would never recognize considerations that have nothing to do with the question of love. The maiden herself is a precious gift. Will you accept it?

Burgundy: If the most gracious king will bestow on her that dowry which he himself offered, I accept her here and now and make her my duchess.

Lear: She shall have no dowry. I have given my word and will not break it.

Burgundy: I greatly regret that, owing to your attitude toward your father, lady, I am unable to remain any longer a suitor for your hand.

Cordelia: Go your way, my lord. Since you are influenced solely by considerations of wealth, I am happy to think that you will be no husband of mine.

France: Lovely maiden, you appear in my sight most richly dowered now that you lack wealth other than yourself, most desirable when others neglect you and worthy of the deepest affection when others hold you in contempt. Let me now take possession of your sweet and virtuous self, for none will hinder me from taking what no one else desires. By heaven! It is almost incredible how my affection has been stimulated by their scorn. This child of yours, Lear, without wealth or possessions, cast off by you, to be wed by any who may choose, I now take as my queen. She shall rule and reign, not only over our lovely land, but over myself, its king, and no lord of Burgundy shall deprive me of this priceless treasure. Cordelia, though they have treated you so ill, bid them adieu. You are leaving your own country to journey to a more desirable land.

Lear: Take her, king; you are welcome to her. She is no child of mine, nor do I ever wish to look upon her again. Therefore, set forth on your journey, but do not expect favor or blessing from me. Let us go, my lord of Burgundy.

[Flourish. Exeunt all but France, Goneril,
Regan and Cordelia.]

France: Take leave of your sisters, Cordelia.

Cordelia: With tear-filled eyes, I say farewell to you, my father's most precious possessions, whom he prizes so greatly. Your real character is well known to me but, as your sister, I am most unwilling to give your faults their true names. Be kind to our dear father. I leave him in your charge, to that love which you have professed for him. If I were still in favor with him, I would commit him to something more worthy of trust. Adieu.

Regan: Do not presume to teach us what we must do.

Goneril: You had better spend your time in trying to please your husband, who has only taken you out of charity. You have not shown a very dutiful affection to our father and do not deserve any other treatment.

Cordelia: The future will bring to light many things now concealed beneath many deceits. Those who try to hide their faults by cunning are generally brought into contempt in the end. Good fortune to you!

France: Come, lovely maid.

[Exeunt France and Cordelia.]

Goneril: Regan, I have a great deal to talk of on a subject which will affect us both very closely. It appears to me that the king intends to depart from here tonight.

Regan: Yes, decidedly. He will accompany you tonight, and, in a month, will come to my house.

Goneril: You have observed how changeable he is in his advancing years. We have often noticed it before. For instance, he cared for Cordelia much more than for us, yet how plainly he has shown what a very little thing was sufficient to make him renounce her.

Regan: This is to be expected from one so old as he is but, even formerly, he seldom was sure of his own mind.

Goneril: Yes, even in his prime he was hasty and reckless. So now, we must expect to find, not only his habitual rashness and changeableness confirmed, but the uncertainties of age and temper in addition.

Regan: We shall probably often see such unexpected and capricious acts as the one we have witnessed today, when he sent the Earl of Kent into exile.

Goneril: The King of France is paying his adieux to him now. Let us agree on a course of action, I beg, for if he still retains his prerogatives as king, with such an uncertain temper, the arrangement he has just made will only bring us trouble.

Regan: We will consider the matter.

Goneril: Consider! We must act at once!

[Exeunt.]

ACT I • SCENE 2

[The Earl of Gloucester's castle.]
[Enter Edmund, with a letter.]

Edmund: I will owe allegiance to no laws but those of nature. I will follow my own will and allow no laws and customs of mankind to thwart my plans. Why should I allow a custom — that of accounting the eldest-born the heir — to condemn me to poverty and the custom of disregarding a natural son to forbid me any hopes of succession? I am as handsome to look at as my brother, Edgar, and my intellect is in no way inferior to his. My father cares as much for me as he does for his heir, Edgar. So, Sir Heir, I shall work to obtain your inheritance. If my plan works, the younger son shall come before the elder, and the lower overtop the higher.

[Enter Gloucester.]

Gloucester: What surprising events have followed each other without any warning! The Earl of Kent is exiled, and the King of France has left the country in anger. Lear has given up his authority and is limited to a certain allowance and has gone from the palace tonight. All this has happened, it seems, almost in a moment. Well, Edmund, have you any tidings?

Edmund: No, sir, if it please you.

[Hiding the letter.]

Gloucester: Why are you so anxious to hide that paper?

Edmund: Nothing fresh has happened, sir.

Gloucester: What letter is that you have?

Edmund: Nothing important, sir.

Gloucester: Indeed! Then why hurry it out of sight so anxiously? "Nothing" does not need to be concealed. If it be "Nothing," there is nothing to see, and, if you let me look at it, I shall be able to read "Nothing" without glasses. Show it to me.

Edmund: Pray forgive me, my lord. The letter is from Edgar, but I have not yet read it all, and, to judge by what I have already seen, it is not right that you should see it.

Gloucester: Let me have it, sir.

Edmund: You will be displeased, whether I keep it or show it to you. That is not my fault, but the fault of the letter, as far as I have grasped its meaning.

Gloucester: Show it to me at once.

Edmund: I hope that Edgar merely wrote this to test my loyalty to you, for his own sake.

Gloucester: *[Reads.]* "The obedience we are compelled to render to our elders is very annoying to those in the flower of their youth. The means to enjoy ourselves are not forthcoming until we are too old to take advantage of them. I am beginning to feel it wearisome, this foolish subjection to the rule of elders, which governs us, not by any strength of its own, but merely as far as we choose to submit to it. When we meet, we will discuss this subject further. If, when our father slumbered, his waking again depended upon me, we should enter on our inheritance at once, and you should share equally with your loving brother. — *Edgar.*"

Indeed! A plot here! "If his waking depended on me, we could enter on our inheritance at once." Could my own child find his heart hard enough to conceive such a thought and his hand cruel enough to set it down! Who gave you this letter, and when?

Edmund: It was not given to me, sir. The writer was too crafty for that. It was thrown into my chamber, where I discovered it.

Gloucester: Do you know whether this is Edgar's handwriting?

Edmund: If the contents of the letter had been good, I should have been ready to take an oath it was his, sir. But as matters stand, I should like to think I am mistaken.

Gloucester: Then you know it to be his.

Edmund: His hand wrote the words, but I hope that his heart never truly meant them.

Gloucester: Has he ever tried to find out your opinion on this matter?

Edmund: He has never asked me openly, but I have frequently heard him say that, in cases where a son has arrived at years of manhood and his father is beginning to grow weak with approaching age, it is only right that the son should have charge both of his parent and his parent's wealth.

Gloucester: The knave! That is exactly the idea contained in this letter. Hateful, abominable wretch! Inhuman creature!

Find him out and seize him! Do you know where to find him?

Edmund: I am not quite sure, sir. But let me beg you to restrain your anger until you have an opportunity of finding out from himself what his real intentions are. Then you will be more certain how to proceed. If you now take severe measures against him, only to find out that you have been entirely mistaken, it will have a very bad effect upon your future authority over him and may give him reason to despise you. I am willing to pledge my life that this was only written to test my love and loyalty and has no further harm in it.

Gloucester: Do you really think that?

Edmund: If you like, my lord, I will bring you to where you can overhear our conversation. We will speak of this matter, and you shall judge, on the evidence of your own ears, his behavior. I can arrange for this at once, before this night shall fall.

Gloucester: It is surely impossible that he should be so wicked.

Edmund: Quite impossible, I am certain.

Gloucester: So inhuman to his own parent, whose affection for him is so true! Powers above! Go, look for him, Edmund, and gain his confidence so that we may find out the truth. I leave the means entirely to your own discretion. I would willingly give up all I possess to have my doubts removed.

Edmund: I will go at once, my lord, and arrange matters in whatever way seems most convenient. When I have arranged all satisfactorily, I will return and let you know.

Gloucester: The eclipses of the sun and moon which have happened recently are forewarnings of evil about to fall upon us. Those who are learned in natural laws are able to explain the causes of them, but the consequences are beyond their power to explain away. After such dreadful events, we see affection losing its warmth, friend forsaking friend and brother quarrelling with brother. Rebellions occur in the towns, and nation wars with nation; loyalty is forgotten, and treachery flourishes in kings' houses; and the ties of affection between child and parent are broken. My own son illustrates this prophecy, for there a child has turned against his parent, and Lear, in behaving with such cruelty, contrary to a parent's natural disposition, illustrates the case of

13

parent against child. Our days of happiness are over. The good old times have gone. Nothing is to be seen and heard but plots, hypocrisy and deceit, which pursue us on our troubled journey towards the tomb. Seek out the traitor, my son. Do it with diligence and you shall profit by it. To think that the faithful and loyal Kent is exiled for being upright and true! Most amazing!

[Exit.]

Edmund: People have a delightfully illogical way of ascribing all their misfortunes to the heavenly bodies when things have gone wrong, frequently through their own imprudent conduct, as if knaves were compelled to be knavish and fools to be foolish by the influence of the heavenly bodies, and people were villains, traitors and robbers through the power of the planets; as if all the sins of the calendar were committed by the compulsion of the stars and every wicked deed and thought were forced upon us by planetary control. My brother... *[Enter Edgar.]* (and here he comes at the exact and opportune moment, like the climax in the old plays). Now that he is here, I must act my part. The signal for my speech is to be dismally dejected and sigh like some poor distracted creature. — Alas! the darkening of the sun and moon foretold these unhappy dissensions! Fa, la, la, la!

Edgar: Well, Edmund, what grave matters are you puzzling over just now?

Edmund: I am pondering over a prophecy I read not long ago of the events which would happen after the eclipses, which occurred lately.

Edgar: Are you really concerning yourself with such tales?

Edmund: But the consequences which were promised, unfortunately, have really followed, I assure you; for instance, the loss of natural affection between father and child, death and famine, the breaking of old friendships, discord throughout the realm, with threats and curses directed against the highest in the land, unfounded distrust, friends sent into exile, disbanding of armies, marriages broken off and a hundred other misfortunes.

Edgar: Since when did you become a student of the stars?

Edmund: An end to this! How long is it since you saw my father?

Edgar: No longer than last night.

14

Edmund: Did you have any conversation with him?

Edgar: Yes, we talked for a couple of hours.

Edmund: Was he quite friendly with you on parting? Did you see no hint of anger, either in his speech or looks?

Edgar: None whatever.

Edmund: Try to remember whether you have displeased him in any way and, in the meantime, let me warn you not to go near him until his anger has had time to cool down, for, just at present, his wrath is so great against you that, if he were to see you, nothing could soften it.

Edgar: Some wretch has been slandering me.

Edmund: That is just what I am afraid of. Restrain yourself, I beg you, until his anger is not so fierce. Let me suggest that you stay at my chamber for the present. I will then let you know when it is safe for you to come before him. Go, I beg you. Here is the key, and, if you come out, carry some weapon with you.

Edgar: A weapon, Edmund!

Edmund: I am counselling you for your own good. Carry a weapon! If no harm is intended toward you, then I am a liar. I have merely told you what I know to be facts, only I have softened them very much in the telling and have not given you any idea of the real dangers which threaten you. Now go, I urge you!

Edgar: Will you let me have news very soon?

Edmund: I am acting entirely in your interests. *[Exit Edgar.]* With an unsuspecting father and a brother too true-hearted to suspect others of deceit, my plans ought to succeed very well. My schemes will prosper easily, while my brother is so confidingly simple. I see exactly how my plan will work and I shall obtain wealth by brains, if I cannot have it by birth. All means are fair to me that I can use for my own ends.

[Exit.]

ACT I • SCENE 3

[The Duke of Albany's palace.]
[Enter Goneril and Oswald, her steward.]

Goneril: Was one of my retainers struck by the king for reproving his jester?

Oswald: He was, madam.

Goneril: My father insults me continually. Time after time,

15

there is some outburst on his part, which causes strife and dissension among us. I will bear it no longer. The knights in his train are becoming unruly, and he himself continually reproaches me for every small offence. On his return from the hunt, I will refuse to see him. You may tell him I am not well. If you should serve him with less care and attention than before, it will not displease me. I will bear the blame.

Oswald: They are returning now, lady. I can hear them.

[Horns within.]

Goneril: Be as disobedient as you will when in attendance on him and tell your fellow-servants to do the same. I prefer the matter to be settled at once. If my father is displeased, he can go to my sister's house. She and I are perfectly agreed on this question and will not give way. He has now too little to occupy him and wishes still to exercise the powers that he delegated to others. When an old man is foolish, he enters upon a second childhood, and when kindness is abused, must be reproved as well as coaxed. Do not forget my instructions.

Oswald: Yes, madam.

Goneril: You can also be more distant in your behavior towards his knights and do not fear, although it may lead to censure. Let my servants know of this, for I wish to bring about an opportunity of letting my father know my mind on this matter. I will send word immediately to my sister, telling her to act in the same way. Now make dinner ready.

[Exeunt.]

ACT I • SCENE 4

[A hall.]
[Enter Kent, disguised.]

Kent: If I can only disguise my voice, as well as my dress, I may succeed in carrying out to its full extent the purpose I had in thus losing my identity. If it should happen that I, the exiled earl, can find an opportunity to be of service to the master who scorned me, though I loved him, that opportunity shall find me ready to toil on his behalf.

[Horns within. Enter Lear, knights and attendants.]

Lear: See that I do not have to wait one instant for dinner. Go

16

and prepare it at once. *[Exit an attendant.]* Well, who are you?

Kent: A man, sir.

Lear: What have you to say of yourself? And what is your business with me?

Kent: I have only the truth to say of myself. I do not wish you to take me for anything which my appearance does not show. I only wish to take service under a master who will trust me, to do my utmost for an honorable man, to be friendly with those who are wise enough not to talk too much, to remember that I must account for my deeds, to fight when I cannot avoid doing so and not to fast on Fridays.

Lear: Who are you?

Kent: A trusty man whose riches are as scanty as the king's.

Lear: If you have as little wealth for one in your station as he has for one in his, you have little indeed. What do you wish?

Kent: Employment.

Lear: Whose employment do you wish to enter?

Kent: Yours.

Lear: Do you know who I am?

Kent: I do not, but I see in your face a quality which I should be willing to obey.

Lear: What quality do you see?

Kent: Power.

Lear: What tasks can you perform?

Kent: I can ride and run. I can be faithful to a trust. I can spoil an elaborate story in repeating it and carry a simple story plainly. I can perform any task that an average man is qualified for. But my best recommendation is my industry.

Lear: What is your age?

Kent: I am too old to fall in love with a woman for her accomplishments and not old enough to lose my wits over her for any reason. My age is forty-eight years.

Lear: Remain among my followers. I will employ you, and, if I am as satisfied with you after dinner as I am at present, you shall stay with me for some time. Ho, there! dinner! Where is my jester? You, sirrah, go and bring him here.

[Exit an attendant.]
[Enter Oswald.]

You, fellow, where is your mistress?

Oswald: If you please . . .

[Exit.]

Lear: What does the rascal say? Bring the clown back.

[Exit a knight.]

Where is my jester? Everyone seems to need awakening!
[Re-enter knight.] Well, where is the cur?

Knight: He says his mistress is not well, your majesty.

Lear: But why did not the villain return when I sent for him?

Knight: My lord, he told me bluntly that he refused to come.

Lear: He refused!

Knight: I cannot tell what is the cause of it, sir, but, in my opinion, your majesty no longer receives the respectful treatment to which you have been accustomed. There is a great falling-off of courtesy and affection observable in the manners of all around us, from Albany himself and his duchess down to the humblest retainer.

Lear: Indeed! Do you think so?

Knight: Pray forgive me, your highness, if I am wrong. I speak because I ought to do so when my master is slighted.

Lear: Your words only serve to recall to my mind what I have myself sometimes thought lately. I have indeed noticed some slight disrespect, but I dismissed it from my mind, as I thought it sprang rather from my own too particular formality than from any intentional offence on the part of others. However, I shall now pursue the matter further. But where is my jester? It is some time since he has been before me.

Knight: He has been drooping, sir, ever since your youngest daughter went away to France.

Lear: Silence, sir, on that subject. I have observed that. Go and say to the Duchess of Albany that I wish to speak to her. *[Exit an attendant.]* You, fellow, tell my jester to come here.

[Exit an attendant.]
[Re-enter Oswald.]

Here, fellow! Come here, sir. Do you know who I am?

Oswald: You are my mistress' father, sir.

Lear: "My mistress' father!" My master's lackey! You wretch! You hound!

Oswald: I am neither wretch nor hound, sir. I beg your pardon!

18

Lear: Do you dare to give me an answer, villain?

[Striking him.]

Oswald: I will not allow you to beat me, sir.

Kent: Nor me to upset you either, I suppose, you stupid footballer!

[Tripping up his heels.]

Lear: Many thanks, good fellow, for your action on my behalf. I like you greatly.

Kent: Now, sir, get up and begone. You shall learn to distinguish things better. Go! If you are anxious to stretch your clownish self on the ground again, then remain here. If not, begone, and quickly! Are you sensible enough to take the hint? Well?

[Pushes Oswald out.]

Lear: Many thanks again, my good fellow. Let this be the first-fruits of your wages.

[Giving Kent money.]
[Enter fool.]

Fool: I'll engage him to my service also. Here is the fool's cap for him.

[Offering Kent his cap.]

Lear: My dear jester, how are you?

Fool: You had better take my fool's cap, fellow.

Kent: Why should I?

Fool: For befriending one who is in disgrace. If you cannot suit your behavior to your company, you will soon be left out in the cold. Here, take my fool's cap. This man you wish to serve has sent two of his children away and given another a blessing most unwillingly. If you serve him, you are certainly a fool. Well, well, master! I wish I had two fool's caps and two daughters.

Lear: Why, my son?

Fool: I think, though, that I should keep the fool's caps myself if I gave everything else I had to my daughters. Here is one from me. Ask your children to give you another.

Lear: Beware of punishment, fool!

Fool: Aye, when Truth speaks, he must be hustled out into the cold, while others, no better behaved, are welcomed round the hearth.

Lear: You mischievous plague!

Fool: You shall learn a speech from me.

Lear: Teach me, then.

Fool: Attend carefully, good uncle: Never show all that you possess and never tell all that you know. Never lend more than you own and never walk when you could ride. Never play for more than you can stake. Do not believe all you learn and you will find that you have more than two tens when you count up your twenty.

Kent: There is nothing in that, fool.

Fool: Then it resembles a speech made by an unpaid lawyer, for you paid nothing for it. My good uncle, could you use nothing?

Lear: Of course not, my lad; there is nothing to use.

Fool: *[To Kent.]* Tell him, will you, that that is exactly the amount he will receive for the rent of his estates. He would refuse to believe a fool.

Lear: A sad jester!

Fool: Do you know, my good man, how a sad fool differs from a merry one?

Lear: I do not, my boy; tell me the difference.

Fool: Let the man who advised you to part with your possessions be made to stand beside me, or shall we say that you represent him? Now, it is easy to see at once the sad fool and the merry one; here am I, the pleasant one, in my motley dress; behold the other!

Lear: Are you saying that I am a fool, then?

Fool: You have not left yourself any other title. But that one must have been yours from birth.

Kent: There is much more than foolishness in this man, your majesty.

Fool: Indeed, I cannot keep all the folly to myself, for the great ones of the land will have some for themselves. Even if I were granted the right to be the sole dealer in it, they would insist on having shares. Even ladies will not leave folly to a jester; they will grasp at it for their own use. Give me an egg, good uncle, and I will return you two crowns.

Lear: What sort of crowns?

Fool: The two empty crowns of the egg, after I have cut it through the center and swallowed all the food to be had out of it. When you divided your egg in two and let other people have both pieces, you were as foolish as the old man in the fable, who carried his ass to please other people. Your respected crown had very little wisdom in it when you parted with your golden one. And if this speech is a fool's speech, I would have the one who discovers it well beaten. *[Singing.]* Never was a time when fools were more foolish, and wise men, too, are anything but wise; they scarcely know what behavior to show, so many tricks they are trying.

Lear: When did you take to making verses, knave?

Fool: I have done it since you, a parent, changed places with your children, when you gave them control over you. *[Singing.]* Then, in delight, they wept aloud, as now I sing in grief that a noble prince should thus run from his position and take his place among fools. I beseech you, good uncle, let me have a teacher. I want to be shown how to avoid speaking the truth.

Lear: If you do not speak the truth, fellow, you shall be flogged.

Fool: I wonder what relationship there can be between you and your daughters. They wish to beat me for speaking the truth, and you threaten to beat me if I do not speak it; and now and then I am beaten for not speaking at all. I would prefer to be anything but what I am. Yet one thing I would not be. I have no wish to be Lear; he has cut away his wisdom in every direction and has none left. Here comes one of the effects of his cutting!

[Enter Goneril.]

Lear: Well, Goneril! Why that expression on your brow? It appears to me that there is too much of this frowning lately.

Fool: You were better off when you were above the necessity of caring whether she frowned or not. Now you are a mere cipher; even I am of more worth. I have at least an acknowledged position, while you have none. *[To Goneril.]* Very well, I will say no more. I can see that you mean it, although you have not spoken. Mum, mum, though one tires of wealth and throws it all away, yet the time will come when it will be longed for. *[Pointing to Lear.]* Behold an empty pod, after the peas have been taken out of it!

Goneril: This fool of yours, sir, who seems to have liberty to say whatever he chooses, is not the only one of your impertinent followers who misbehaves. Others of your train are continually wrangling and rioting and making disturbances that cannot be endured. At first, my lord, I thought that to mention this matter to you would be quite sufficient in order to have it rectified. But now I am inclined to fear, judging by your recent words and actions, that this lawless behavior of your followers is encouraged by you and is continued with your consent. Should that be the case, remember that such offence will not escape punishment, and certain measures might, in the interests of the public good, have to be taken, which possibly might not be to your liking, even such measures as would, under other circumstances, seem oppressive but, in the present case, would be merely prudent.

Fool: Do you not know what happens to the hedge-sparrow when it has reared and fed a young cuckoo? How the cuckoo destroys its benefactor at last? So there we are, left without light!

Lear: Is this my child?

Goneril: I wish, my lord, that you would call to your aid the good sense that I know you possess and indulge no more in these wayward humors, which alter you so much from your usual self.

Fool: Any donkey can see when the driver is driven! Ha, ha! How dear thou art to me!

Lear: Is there anyone here who can tell me who I am? Surely I cannot be the king! Is it Lear who speaks in this way? Are these his limbs, or his eyes? Either his mind is giving way, his faculties are stupefied, or — surely I cannot be awake! I am dreaming, am I not? Will someone tell me who I am?

Fool: The phantom of a king!

Lear: I wish to know, for my senses and position seem to tell me that I had daughters.

Fool: And well they will teach their father to obey!

Lear: Fair lady, what are you called?

Goneril: This pretended amazement, my lord, is quite in keeping with other performances of yours lately. Pray attend to me and try to understand my intentions. You should have some wisdom, being an aged and venerable man. You number in your train five-score knights and squires. These men are so wild and lawless that, by their example, this palace is more like a public inn, where gluttony and vice reigns, than the dwelling of princes. This disgraceful state of things must be remedied at once, so I beg you to do as I ask, so that I may not be obliged to force it upon you. My request is that you reduce the number of your followers and let the men you keep as your retainers be serious and wise and old enough to know both their place and yours.

Lear: Fiends of black night! To horse! Summon my followers! I will leave you instantly. You are no child of mine, but I have yet a child remaining!

Goneril: My people have been beaten by your hand, and your unruly mob tries to rule those who are better than themselves.

[Enter Albany.]

Lear: Alas! for him who regrets after the deed is done!
[To Albany.] Are you there, my lord? Is this to your mind? Answer me! Bring out the steeds. O what an unfeeling monster is thanklessness, when shown by children to parents — more dreadful than the frightful sea monster!

Albany: Calm yourself, I beseech you, sir.

Lear: *[To Goneril.]* Hateful creature! It is false. The knights in my retinue are men of the greatest excellencies and fairest qualities, men who are most scrupulous in their behavior and who know well how to bear themselves, who have too much regard for their own reputation and honor to degrade themselves by any lawlessness. How little does Cordelia's offence appear now, though like a rack it tore my heart and altered my disposition towards her at the time. It quenched my love and filled my heart with bitterness. O foolish Lear, beat at that head, which welcomed madness and drove away discretion! *[Striking his head.]* Come, my knights, let us depart.

Albany: I am innocent, sir, of any offence toward you. Neither do I know what has thus stirred your feelings.

Lear: That is very possible, sir. Listen, O goddess of nature; hearken to my words! If thy intention was to bless this being with offspring, arrest now in her all power to bring this to pass. Never may such a degraded creature be the happy parent of a child to hold her in reverence! Or, if this may not be, then let her child be altogether evil. May it grow in unnatural perversity. May her cheeks be lined by misery and bitter, falling tears before ever they are lined by age. May all her kindnesses and toil be made a mockery of, and let her heart be pierced, as mine has been, by a sting far keener than that of the serpent — the ingratitude of a child! Away! Let us depart!

[Exit.]

Albany: Heavenly powers above! What is the cause of this?

Goneril: Do not trouble yourself about that, but let the natural waywardness of old age have its way.

[Re-enter Lear.]

Lear: Is it possible? Fifty of my train dismissed at one stroke! And this in less than two weeks from the time I gave you all!

Albany: What is your grievance my lord?

Lear: I'll tell you! *[To Goneril.]* Life and death! I scorn myself that your insults should affect me so much and that this rush of scalding tears, beyond my control for the moment, seems a tribute to your power to wound. Blight and destruction fall upon you!

May the curse of an outraged parent stab you to the very soul, beyond power to fathom! If my foolish old eyes shed another tear on your account, I will tear them from their place and fling them to the ground to water it with their moisture. Can this be really so? Well, no matter! I have yet another child. She will certainly comfort me and show me love and will be ready to tear your cruel features with her own hands when she knows the treatment I have received from you. You shall see me soon restored to that position which you now think I have irrevocably lost. I promise you, you shall see it!

[Exeunt Lear, Kent and attendants.]

Goneril: Well, sir, do you see that?

Albany: Goneril, I cannot let my affection for you blind me to . . .

Goneril: That will do. Oswald, Oswald! *[To the fool.]* You, sir, less fool than villain, begone with him you serve!

Fool: Lear, good uncle Lear, wait and let your fool accompany you. Foxes that are hunted and daughters that are cruel should all be slain if a coxcomb would pay for the rope. So away I go after my master.

[Exit.]

Goneril: He was well advised indeed. Five-score knights

24

indeed! Oh! no doubt it was the height of wisdom to let him keep five-score, well-armed knights about him, and at every turn, every whim, every caprice, every fancied grievance, they are at hand to enforce the whims of his old age and keep us entirely in his power.

Albany: You may carry your mistrust of him too far.

Goneril: That is better than to be too confident. I prefer to prevent the dangers I foresee, not to live in dread of their coming. I know my father's nature. I have sent an account to Regan of all that he has said. If she agrees to maintain him with all his train after I have pointed out to her the unsuitability . . .

[Re-enter Oswald.]

Well, Oswald, is that message to my sister prepared?

Oswald: It is, my lady.

Goneril: Mount at once, then, and take someone with you. Tell her fully of the circumstances and what I am afraid will happen and add anything you may think of to the story to confirm and corroborate it. Go quickly and return as speedily as possible.

[Exit Oswald.]

No, no, Albany, I do not blame you for the milder course you wish to take or for the softness of your heart. But, if you will forgive me, you are oftener burdened with foolish timidity than approved of because of your gentleness.

Albany: I cannot say what dangers you may foresee, but I know that sometimes matters are made worse by trying to improve them.

Goneril: Not at all.

Albany: But no matter, time will show.

[Exeunt.]

ACT I • SCENE 5

[Court before the same.]
[Enter Lear, Kent and fool.]

Lear: Go on ahead of us and carry this message to the Earl of Gloucester. Say nothing to Regan about anything which has occurred. Merely answer any questions she may ask you after reading the letter. Ride quickly or you will not arrive sooner than I.

Kent: I will give the letter safely into Gloucester's hand before I take any rest.

[Exit.]

Fool: If a person's wits lay in his feet, would they not be apt to get frostbitten?

Lear: To be sure, my lad.

Fool: Then you have no cause for sadness, for yours do not lie there; your wits will never be down at heel!

Lear: Ha, ha, ha!

Fool: You will receive much kindness at the hands of Regan. She is as like her sister as two kinds of apples are like each other. Yet I know what I know.

Lear: What do you know, my lad?

Fool: If they were both sampled, they would both be found equally sour! Why is a man's nose in the middle of his face?

Lear: I do not know.

Fool: So that he may have an eye on each side. Then, when his nose fails to serve him, his eyes are ready to be on the lookout.

Lear: I was too hasty with Cordelia.

Fool: Do you know how an oyster makes its shell?

Lear: I do not.

Fool: Neither do I, but I can tell you why a snail has a shell of his own.

Lear: Why?

Fool: To live in it himself, not to part with it to his daughters and leave himself without a hole to hide his head in.

Lear: I am tempted to act unnaturally. How could she do it to such a generous father! Are the horses ready yet?

Fool: They are being got ready by your donkeys. It is an excellent reason, which makes the seven stars only seven.

Lear: Is it because they are not eight?

Fool: Exactly. You would make an excellent fool.

Lear: To compel me to give them up! Such ingratitude is almost incredible!

Fool: You should be whipped, good uncle, if you were my jester, for reaching old age too soon.

Lear: What do you mean?

Fool: You should not have reached old age till you had reached wisdom.

26

Lear: O kind heaven, keep me from going mad! Keep me sane. Let me not lose my senses. Surely I am not mad!

[Enter gentleman.]

Well, is all in readiness to mount?

Gentleman: All is prepared, sir.

Lear: Let us go, my lad.

ACT II • SCENE 1

[The Earl of Gloucester's castle.]
[Enter Edmund, and Curan meets him.]

Edmund: Good day, Curan.

Curan: Good day to you, sir. I have just been to inform the Earl of Gloucester that he will have guests at the castle tonight: the Duke and Duchess of Cornwall.

Edmund: Why are they coming here?

Curan: That I cannot tell. I suppose you know the rumors that are being repeated. I mean the secret tidings, for they are not yet spoken of openly.

Edmund: I know nothing. Let me hear the news, pray.

Curan: Have no whispers reached you of quarrels between the two husbands of the king's daughters — quarrels which may lead to fighting very soon?

Edmund: I have not heard a syllable.

Curan: It will probably not be long until you do. Adieu, sir.

[Exit.]

Edmund: Cornwall here tonight! That is all the better; in fact, the best that could possibly happen for my plans! Everything is working to further my ends. My father's men are on the watch for Edgar, and now I have a delicate piece of work before me, which must be done at once. May speed and good luck be mine! Edgar, I want to speak with you. Come down, Brother. Edgar!

[Enter Edgar.]

Escape from here quickly. Someone has told my father where you are concealed, and his men are watching for you, but the darkness of the night may aid your escape. Have you been saying anything which could offend the Duke of Cornwall? He is expected here this very night and he seems to have some reason for haste. His wife is coming also. Or have you been taking his part against the Duke of Albany? Do you think you are safe there? Consider!

Edgar: I have said nothing whatever; of that I am certain.

Edmund: My father is approaching. Forgive me, but I must pretend to be fighting with you. Come, draw your sword and pretend to engage against me. Make a brave show! Now, surrender and let me take you before him. Bring lights, there! Now is your time to escape, Edgar! Bring lights, torches! There, now good-bye.

[Exit Edgar.]

If I appeared to be wounded, it would seem to prove that I had fought more desperately. *[Wounds his arm.]* I have seen people do more harm to themselves in mere drunken sport. Father! Father! Stop, villain! Will no one help me?

[Enter Gloucester and servants, with torches.]

Gloucester: Where is he, Edmund? Where is the knave?

Edmund: He was standing here, to attack me in the darkness, his keen weapon ready drawn, while he muttered unholy spells and called on the moon to be favorable to his exploits!

Gloucester: But where is he?

Edmund: See, my lord, I am wounded.

Gloucester: Where is the knave now?

Edmund: He escaped in that direction. When he found it was impossible . . .

Gloucester: Follow after him, there!

[Exeunt some servants.]

When it was impossible to do what?

Edmund: To induce me to agree to kill you, sir. When I spoke to him of the horror in which the gods hold those who slay their parents and of the terrible vengeance by which they are pursued, and when I reminded him of the holy ties which bind parents and children together as with powerful cords, then, my lord, when he at length saw with what abhorrence I turned from his monstrous design, he fiercely attacked me with his already drawn weapon, while I stood defenceless before him. He wounded me in the arm; but, whether he was surprised by my spirited defence of myself in such a righteous cause, or whether terror-stricken when I called out for help, I know not. But he ran hastily away.

Gloucester: He must flee a long way if he wishes to remain in safety, for nowhere throughout this whole realm will he be able to escape capture, and, when captured, then slain! The worthy Cornwall, my chief, is to arrive here tonight, and I shall get him to lend his sanction to a proclamation that whoever secures the villain Edgar will be doing me a service, if he brings the guilty wretch to punishment, and whoever helps him to remain hidden from me will be punished with death.

Edmund: When I attempted to turn him from his purpose and discovered that he was firmly resolved upon it, I spoke to him harshly and said that I would expose him, but he answered, "Do you imagine, you penniless, base-born wretch, that if I chose to contradict your story anyone would be found to repose sufficient faith in you to credit your word? It is not likely, and all that you accused me of — as of course I should deny that I had ever suggested this, even though you could produce my handwriting in proof of it — I should convert into evidence against you and say that you yourself had laid the plot and arranged the plans, and people would have to be very stupid indeed not to see clearly how my death would benefit you and how very strongly self-interest would urge you on to seek those advantages which my death would give you."

Gloucester: The hardened wretch! Would he even swear his own handwriting was not his! He is no child of mine! *[Tucket within.]* There are Cornwall's bugles. His errand here is a mystery to me! I will close all the ways of escape, so that the knave cannot get free. The duke will consent to that, and Edgar's likeness shall also be sent over all the country, so that he may be recognized and captured. As for you, my faithful child, I shall take steps to make you my lawful heir.

[Enter Cornwall, Regan and attendants.]

Cornwall: What is this, my good Gloucester? I have heard strange tidings since I came, though I have only just arrived.

Regan: The heaviest punishment is too light for such an offence, if what we hear is true. How are you, sir?

Gloucester: My heart is broken — broken, lady!

Regan: Can it be that the boy to whom Lear stood sponsor would seek to slay his father!

Gloucester: Ah! madam, gladly would I conceal it, for very shame's sake!

Regan: He was much in the company of those lawless knights of my father's train, was he not?

Gloucester: I cannot say, lady. It is dreadful, terrible!

Edmund: Yes, noble lady, he often made one of that company.

Regan: Then it is no wonder that he is evilly disposed. It is those wicked men who have instigated his plans against his father, in order to have the disposal of his wealth. This very

evening, my sister has sent me such news of them, warning
me of their behavior so that I do not intend to receive them
at my castle. If they come there, I shall be purposely absent.

Cornwall: So shall I, Regan, be sure. I am told, Edmund, that
you have nobly acted a son's part towards your father.

Edmund: It was only right that I should, sir.

Gloucester: Yes, he exposed the villain's plot and was
wounded, as you may see, in trying to arrest him.

Cornwall: Have you sent anyone after him?

Gloucester: Yes, noble sir.

Cornwall: You will never again need to fear any injury from
him, once he is captured. You may do to him what you will,
with my full permission and authority. As for you,
Edmund, I appreciate so heartily your goodness and loyalty
at this time that I shall take you into my service. I am likely
to be in need of men whose trustworthiness I can rely on,
and you shall be one of the first appointed.

Edmund: My service, sir, shall at least be faithful, whatever else
it may be.

Gloucester: I am grateful also, my lord, on his behalf.

Cornwall: You do not yet know the reason for our visit.

Regan: At this untimely hour, in the gloom of night, events are
happening, my lord, events of some weight, on which we
need your wisdom and counsel to guide us. We have
received messages, both from my father and from Goneril,
telling of quarrels and strife, and it seemed to me that it
would be better to send the answers from some other place
rather than our own palace. Both the messengers are here,
awaiting our replies. Be comforted, our dear and worthy
friend, and give us your advice on this matter, which is
very urgent.

Gloucester: I am entirely at your service, lady, and bid you both
heartily welcome.

[Flourish. Exeunt.]

ACT II • SCENE 2

[Before Gloucester's castle.]
[Enter Kent and Oswald, severally.]

Oswald: Good morrow, friend. Do you belong to this castle?

Kent: I do.

Oswald: Where may we stable our horses?

31

Kent: In the mud.

Oswald: Tell me, I pray, if you have any kindness.

Kent: I have none for you.

Oswald: Well, then, I do not need you.

Kent: If I got you in Lipsbury pound, I would make you heed me.

Oswald: Why do you treat me in this way? I do not know you.

Kent: But I am acquainted with you, sirrah.

Oswald: And what is your knowledge of me?

Kent: That you are a knave, a scoundrel, a feeder on scraps, a low, conceited, empty-headed creature, the poorest of the poor, among gentlemen or servingmen, a cowardly wretch, settling your quarrels by an action at law, an affected, foppish dandy, a creature who will do any base service that's required and is a cowardly, base-born creature himself and one that I will whip until he howls, if he dares say I lie in any of the titles I have given him!

Oswald: What an atrocious creature! Why do you heap these insults on me, who do not even know who you are, and who is equally unknown to you?

Kent: And what an insolent lackey are you to say that you do not know me! It is not so very long ago that I overthrew you and thrashed you in the presence of King Lear. Out with your sword, knave, and fight, for there is moonlight enough to fight by. I'll make a hash of you! Fight, you cowardly fop!

[Drawing his sword.]

Oswald: Begone! I will not concern myself with you.

Kent: Fight, villain! You have brought messages to the injury of his kingly dignity. Fight, you rascal or I'll carve you. Come on!

Oswald: Help! Murder! Help!

Kent: Fight, you coward. Stand, stand, rascal. Fight, you slave!

[Beating him.]

Oswald: Help! I shall be killed! Help!

[Enter Edmund, with his rapier drawn, Cornwall, Regan, Gloucester and servants.]

Edmund: Now, then! What is all this about?

[Parting them.]

Kent: I'll take you, master youth. Come on. I'll give you a chance to use your maiden sword. Come your ways, boy!

Gloucester: Swords drawn here! What is this?

Cornwall: Cease this brawling, on pain of death! The next one who strikes a blow shall die. What is the quarrel?

Regan: Why, they are the men who brought the letters from my father and Goneril!

Cornwall: What have you quarrelled about? Come, let us hear.

Oswald: I have scarcely breath to answer, sir.

Kent: It is no wonder, seeing how valiantly you fought! You timid slave, nature disowns you. You must have been cut out by a tailor!

Cornwall: You are an odd creature! Cut out by a tailor?

Kent: Yes, sir, for neither a mason nor a painter could have turned out such a wretched figure of a man, even if they had been only beginners.

Cornwall: But go on to the cause of your disagreement.

Oswald: This rascal, my lord, whose gray hairs induced me to spare his life . . .

Kent: You useless creature! If you, sir, would allow me, I would break this coarse wretch up into a heap of lime and use him to whitewash outhouses! You jackanapes! Spare me, indeed, on account of my grey hairs!

Cornwall: Silence, fellow! Have you no regard for decent behavior, you savage creature?

Kent: Yes, my lord, but an angry man is allowed some licence.

Cornwall: What caused your anger?

Kent: Seeing a lying, deceitful villain like this, allowed to wear the appearance of an honest gentleman. It is just such fair-faced, smooth-tongued scoundrels as this who often, like the vermin they are, help to gnaw apart the most closely twined bonds of virtue and affection, which would otherwise hold firm and strong. They are ready to excuse and gloss over every misdeed and indiscretion of their masters, to inflame their rage, or to add coldness to their displeasure, to deny anything, or agree with anything which will suit their lords, and turn their faces back or forward, like the poor kingfisher hung up for a weathercock, according to every mood and whim of those they serve. Ignorant themselves, they blindly follow their leader, as do their hounds. Curses on your distorted face! Do you sneer at what I say, as if I were an imbecile? If I once got you on Salisbury Plain, where geese like you are herded, you would soon be driven quacking home to Camelot.

Cornwall: Are you out of your mind, man?

Gloucester: Tell us at once what led to this quarrel.

Kent: You could not find any opposing elements so antagonistic to each other as this villain and I.

Cornwall: Why do you say he is a villain? What fault has he committed?

Kent: His face does not please me.

Cornwall: Neither does mine, very probably, nor these others you see.

Kent: It is my business to speak plainly, my lord, and I agree that the faces I see around me at present are certainly less pleasing than some I have known.

Cornwall: This man has evidently, at some time, been commended for his blunt manner of speech, and so he puts on a showy kind of rudeness and pretends to an abruptness and rudeness which he really does not feel. It is all done as a pose. He will never soil his tongue by flattery, not he! He is a blunt, plain-spoken man, and, if people like to hear the truth, well and good, they will get it from him. If not, then so much the worse for them. They will still get it. There are no deceits and smooth phrases about him! I know this sort of specimen, these fellows who, under the guise of blunt, honest, truth-telling, conceal more cunning tricks and evil deeds than a score of bowing, smirking, watchful courtiers, openly ready to please their lords with the greatest diligence.

Kent: My lord, in candid truth, in genuine veracity, by permission of your most noble presence, which sheds its rays like the radiance of the glorious beams which illuminate the glowing face of the sun god . . .

Cornwall: What in the world is all this about?

Kent: I am merely changing my style of conversation, as my ordinary speech seems to displease you so much. At the same time, I am not double-tongued. If you have been deceived by a bluntly spoken man, then, to speak as bluntly, he was a villain, and that I refuse to be, even though you should, in spite of your dislike of me, wish me to be one.

Cornwall: What did you do to offend him?

Oswald: Nothing whatever. The king, whom he serves, was not

34

long ago pleased to deal me a blow on account of some misunderstanding, when this fellow, in agreement with the king's mood and encouraging his anger, laid me by the heels. Then, when I was down, he abused me and heaped insults upon me and altogether made such a brave show that he was greatly exalted in the king's eyes and won much commendation for so valiantly attacking one who was offering no resistance. The glory of this courageous feat has so dazzled him that he attacked me again just now.

Kent: The exploits of the valiant Greek before Troy are foolish, compared with the boastings of these cowardly rascals!

Cornwall: You obstinate old villain, you grey-headed boaster! You shall be taught a lesson. Let the stocks be brought for him!

Kent: I cannot be taught new lessons at my time of life, so spare your trouble and bring no stocks for me. I am the king's messenger and engaged on his errand here. It would be insolence, indeed, and greatly lacking in the honor due to his royal dignity to place his envoy in the stocks.

Cornwall: Bring them here, I say! As I am a living man, I swear by my faith that he shall be locked into them until midday.

Regan: Until midday? Say rather until evening and until next morning!

Kent: Such treatment, lady, is not fitting, even for one of your father's hounds.

Regan: It shall be fitting, however, for my father's lackey.

Cornwall: This is exactly the kind of behavior of which Goneril has told us. Come, fetch the stocks here!

[Stocks brought out.]

Gloucester: I beg of you, my lord, not to do this. He certainly has offended greatly and he will be reproved for it by our noble king. The punishment you are intending for him is most shameful and only used for the most base creatures to punish the meanest faults. The king will be greatly displeased to find that anyone thinks so lightly of his dignity as to confine his messenger in so disgraceful a position.

Cornwall: I will be responsible for that.

Regan: My sister will very probably be still more highly displeased when she finds that her messenger has been attacked and insulted while engaged in her concerns. Lock him in safely.

Come, Cornwall, let us go.

[Exeunt all but Gloucester and Kent.]

Gloucester: I am grieved for your sake, sir, but everyone knows that it is impossible to turn the duke aside from anything he has resolved upon, and he has chosen to do this. But I will say what I can on your behalf.

Kent: Do not trouble, my lord. I am tired out with travelling and weary for lack of sleep, so I shall pass some of the time in slumber and whistle for the rest. Everyone is unlucky at some time or other, even the best of us. Good day to you, my lord.

Gloucester: The duke's conduct is very wrong. The king will be greatly displeased.

[Exit.]

Kent: I can see, noble Lear, that you are about to prove the truth of the old saying — "Out of God's benison into the warm sun," and go from better to worse. Light of this lower globe rise, that by your comforting rays I may see to read this letter. Miracles seldom happen, except in extreme wretchedness. This, I know, is sent by Cordelia. By great good fortune, she has heard of my being under a cloud at present and, out of this monstrous state of affairs, she will, no doubt, bring some order and repair some of these crying wrongs. Weary eyes, tired-out with wakeful hours, now take this opportunity of closing, and the sight of this undignified resting-place will no longer offend you. Look kindly on me, fortune, and so good-night. Let thy wheel spin round to favor me once more.

[Sleeps.]

ACT II • SCENE 3

[A wood.]

[Enter Edgar.]

Edgar: I heard the announcement proclaiming me an outlaw but, by means of a hiding-place, which I fortunately found in a hollow tree, I have evaded those who pursued me. There is no place in which I may shelter myself, no refuge left. In every place, I am searched for, and the most strict watch is kept so that I may be captured. I will protect myself as long as possible and keep safely out of my enemies' way while I can. I think it would be wise to assume the meanest disguise possible and put on the lowest appearance that ever a human being was compelled to by poverty. I will soil my face and mat my hair into tangled untidiness, wrap merely a cloth around my body and, for the rest, go naked to the weather and brave the worst that wind and rain can do. Instances are not lacking to prove that this can be done, for many mad creatures roam about the land, shouting and injuring themselves with sharp-pointed things with which they pierce their flesh, deadened with cold. Thus, wandering from one poor farm or petty hamlet to another, by mills and shepherds' huts, they induce the poor folk to give them alms by the sight of their injuries, by wild, mad curses or by their prayers and pleadings. Poor Turlygod! Poor Tom! That is what I am now. I am Edgar no longer.

[Exit.]

ACT II • SCENE 4
[Before Gloucester's castle, Kent in the stocks.]
[Enter Lear, fool and gentleman.]

Lear: I cannot understand their leaving home in this way, without sending me any reply by my messenger.

Gentleman: I found out that, only on the evening before, they had no intention of leaving home so suddenly.

Kent: Greeting, most noble king!

Lear: Ha! Have you taken up this disgraceful position in jest?

Kent: No, your majesty.

Fool: Ha! Ha! His legs are bound with "crewel" work. One ties a horse by the head, a dog or bear is led by the neck, a monkey by a string round its waist and a man is fastened by the leg. And if a man's legs lead him into mischief, then he is provided with stockings made of wood.

Lear: Who is the man who has so far forgotten your position as to place you here?

Kent: It was both a man and a woman: your daughter and her husband did it.

Lear: You do not mean that.

Kent: I do.

Lear: I say it is impossible!

Kent: I say it is true!

Lear: They would never do so.

Kent: They have done it.

Lear: I vow by the gods, it cannot be!

Kent: And I swear by the goddesses, it is so!

Lear: Surely they would not dare! It is impossible! It is an unheard-of insult, deliberately to offer you this indignity. Tell me as quickly as you reasonably can how it has happened and under what circumstances you, my messenger and servant, could possibly merit, or they could possibly inflict, such treatment.

Kent: When I reached their castle, sir, and had delivered your majesty's letters to your daughter and her husband, I had scarcely risen from my knees where I had bowed before them, when there arrived a perspiring, panting courier with greetings from his mistress, Goneril. He gave them his letters, notwithstanding the fact that mine came first, and they read them at once. On learning the contents of the letters, they immediately prepared to ride away, with all their attendants. I was told to follow them and wait until they could spare time to reply to my message. They looked upon me with great disfavor, and, when we arrived here, I met again with Goneril's servant, whose message, I saw, had been the cause of their coolness towards me, and I found that he was none other than the man who behaved so insolently to your majesty only a short time ago. With more courage than wisdom, I drew my sword upon him, whereupon, with noisy cries, he called out, like a coward, for help and brought everyone out to see what the disturbance was about. The duke and his wife then decided that my offence deserved this punishment which you see.

Fool: There is more bad weather to come, if that is the direction of the wild bird's flight. When parents are poverty-stricken, their children ignore them. It is parents who are wealthy who have loving children. Yet, I can promise you, you shall have as many sorrows for your daughters as you can count in a year.

Lear: My rising grief threatens to overwhelm me. Subside passionate sorrow! Let me restrain myself. Where is this child of mine?

Kent: In the castle here, sir, with her husband.

Lear: Remain outside. Let me go in alone.

[Exit.]

38

Gentleman: Have you displeased them in any other way than the one you have told us?

Kent: No. How is it that there are so few knights in attendance on the king?

Fool: Now, if that question had been what caused you to be put in the stocks, it would have been no more than you deserved.

Kent: How is that?

Fool: You will have to go to the ant to learn the lesson that it is only when the sun shines that one can provide for the winter. Every man is led by appearances, except those who cannot see, and even they can tell without difficulty when a man is out of favor. Never try to cling tightly to a great one going downhill. You will only run the risk of being broken yourself. But if there should be a great one ascending, make that the means of pulling you up also. If any man can give you better advice, then let me have mine back again. I would not ask any but knaves to follow it, since it is given by a fool. The man who only seeks for his own advancement and serves his master only in name will soon depart when troubles begin to appear. Fair-weather friends flee before winter's storms. But I, the fool, will face the storm, no matter how many wise men flee. The knave who runs away is a fool, but the fool is no knave, in faith.

Kent: Where were you taught that, fool?

Fool: Not where you are now, fool!

[Re-enter Lear, with Gloucester.]

Lear: They refuse to see me, you say? They are not well and are fatigued with their journey and with lack of rest? These are only excuses, signs and tokens of disobedience and desertion. Let me hear a different reply from this.

Gloucester: Your majesty, you know the Duke of Cornwall's hot-tempered disposition and how impossible it is to persuade him to anything he does not wish to do.

Lear: Vengeance! Plague! Death! Confusion! Hot-tempered, indeed! Disposition! Do you understand, my lord, that I wish to speak to my daughter, Regan, and her husband?

Gloucester: Indeed, your majesty, I have let them know that such is your pleasure.

Lear: Let them know! Have you not comprehended my order?

Gloucester: Yes, your highness.

Lear: It is the king who wishes to speak to his subject, the Duke of Cornwall. It is the father who wishes to see his daughter and whose order it is that she shall attend him! And you have "let them know!" On my life! Hot-tempered! The hot-tempered duke! Say to the fiery duke that — but wait! I will wait awhile. It is just possible he may be sick, and, in ill-health, we are all apt to disregard the duties which we should readily discharge when in good health. In times of sickness, when the weakness of the body reacts upon the mind, we are unlike our usual selves and act as we should not do upon ordinary occasions. I will restrain myself. I now reproach myself for my impetuous haste in expecting a sick man to behave in all respects as one in good health would do. *[Looking at Kent.]* But, by my kingdom, why is he placed there? Now that I consider that action, I am convinced that this hasty journey of Cornwall and his wife and their persisent absenting of themselves from my presence are parts of an arranged plan. Release my messenger at once and say to my daughter and her husband that I desire to see them without delay. They are to come immediately and speak with me or I will raise a cry at their door that will give them no rest till they appear.

Gloucester: I hope that there will be no quarrel between you. I desire nothing better than that you should be at peace with each other.

[Exit.]

Lear: Oh! how my bosom swells! But I will repress it.

Fool: Yes, good uncle, command it to keep its place, as the cook did to the eels when she put them into a pie without killing them first. She rapped them on the head with a stick and told them to keep down. It was one of the same family that buttered his horse's hay, out of sheer goodness of heart.

[Re-enter Gloucester, with Cornwall, Regan and servants.]

Lear: Good day to you, Regan and Cornwall.

Cornwall: Greeting, my lord!

[Kent is set at liberty.]

Regan: I am happy to see you, your majesty.

Lear: I believe that you mean this. I have good reason to expect it of you and, if I thought that by any chance it should not be true, I should have to disown your mother's grave and believe that you were no child of mine! *[To Kent.]* Ah!

They have released you. I shall speak of that matter later. Dear Regan, your sister, Goneril, has proved herself to be a worthless creature. O my daughter, she has planted the sting of keenest ingratitude in my bosom. *[Points to his heart.]* My tongue refuses to repeat her unkindnesses. You could never even credit what disgraceful — O my child!

Regan: Let me beg of you, my lord, not to find fault too readily. I trust that we shall find it is you who do not rightly appreciate her, rather than she who fails in her duty towards you.

Lear: In what way can that be so?

Regan: I am unable to believe that Goneril would fail in her duty. If, as is probably the case, she may have checked the lawless behavior of your train, it is for such good reason that you cannot hold her to blame in the matter.

Lear: My curses on her!

Regan: My lord, your years are many. You have reached almost to the farthest bounds of the span of life, and now it is fitting that you should be guided by a stronger and wiser mind, more capable of judging rightly of your welfare than you yourself can do. For that reason, let me beg you to go back to my sister, Goneril, and acknowledge that you have been mistaken.

Lear: Ask pardon of Goneril? See, then, what a fitting petition it would be! *[Kneeling.]* "Most loving child, your father acknowledges the fact of his old age. An aged man is a burden, and a needless one. I therefore kneel to you and beg the favor of a resting-place, together with food and clothing."

Regan: That will do, sir; these antics are most unbecoming. Let me advise you to go back to Goneril.

Lear: *[Rising.]* I will never do that! She has diminished my retinue to half its size, frowned upon me in displeasure and wounded my very soul with her stinging words. May all the punishments the gods can send fall upon her ungrateful head! Ye blasting winds, cripple her youthful frame!

Cornwall: For shame, my lord!

Lear: Flash your searing fires, swift lightnings, into her haughty eyes, and ye marshy airs, sucked from the poisonous swamp, strike her with disfiguring sickness and humble her arrogance and pride!

Regan: O divine powers! This is what I may expect when your anger shall be turned against me.

Lear: No, my daughter, my curses shall never be pronounced against you. Your heart, in which dwells tenderness, would never allow you to be swayed by cruelty. Your sister's eyes are hard and pitiless, but yours glow soft and kindly and do not flame in anger. Your nature lacks the harshness that would withhold from me any indulgence. You would never reduce the number of my attendants, pick quarrels with me, reprove me or deny my allowances, and, finally, refuse me entrance into your dwelling. You are more sensible of the obligations due from child to parent, the natural regard of daughter for father, all that belongs to courtesy and the gratitude which you owe to me. You still remember that I bestowed upon you half of my realm.

Regan: I remember it to good purpose.

Lear: Who ordered my servant to be placed in the stocks?

[Tucket within.]

Cornwall: Whose bugle-call is that?

Regan: I recognize it. It is Goneril's. This agrees with what she wrote to us, that she would visit us shortly.

[Enter Oswald.]

Has your mistress arrived?

Lear: This fellow is a lackey whose haughty insolence is put on because his mistress chooses to regard him with favor. Begone, sirrah! Out of my presence!

Cornwall: Why this outburst, my lord?

Lear: Who gave orders for my man to be confined in the stocks? Surely, my daughter, you knew nothing of it? Who is this approaching?

[Enter Goneril.]

O powers above, if you care for the aged, if your beneficent rule approves of obedience, if you yourselves have seen length of years, befriend me! Stoop down and fight on my side! *[To Goneril.]* Do you not feel shame when you see my gray hairs again? O Regan, can you greet her in sisterly kindness?

Goneril: Why should she not, my lord? What fault have I committed? Everything that old age calls an offence and that foolish people think wrong, is not really so.

Lear: Give way, my poor frame, give way! Do you still confine my bursting heart? Why was my servant placed in the stocks?

Cornwall: By my orders, my lord, though his behavior deserved a worse position.

Lear: It was your orders? Yours?

Regan: Let me beseech you, sir, to let your behavior be more in accordance with your position. If you will go back now with my sister, Goneril, and, with fifty knights, remain with her until the four weeks are past that were agreed upon, then I shall be glad to receive you. You cannot come to my house now, as I am not only absent myself, but have not yet provided for the reception of so large a number.

Lear: Go back to Goneril, with only half my train? Before I will consent to that, I will dwell under the open sky and commit myself to the elements, contending against their fury with what success I may, with the beasts of the field for my companions, driven by the stern whip of necessity! Go back with Goneril? I could as easily compel myself to kneel at the feet of the fiery prince who wedded my child, Cordelia, portionless, and there beg him, like any servant, for his charity to save me from starvation. Go back with Goneril? Ask me first to be the lackey of, and bear the burdens for, this hateful servant of hers!

[Pointing at Oswald.]

Goneril: As you will, my lord.

Lear: I beseech of you, do not drive me out of my senses! I will be a burden to you no longer, but will bid you adieu, and we will never look upon each other again. But that cannot break the bond between us, cannot alter the fact that you are my child, my own flesh and blood; though indeed you are rather to be compared to an unwholesome outbreak of disease, which yet I must acknowledge as part of me. But I will heap no more reproaches upon you, nor wish for humiliation to overtake you. Let that happen, as it will happen, in its own due time. I will not call down upon you the lightning-shafts of Jove, or make complaint of you to the impartial gods. Do better as you are able, improve and amend your ways when you will. I can wait. I can remain contentedly with my other child, who will welcome me and my train.

Regan: That can scarcely be, my lord. I had not expected you for some time yet and have not made the necessary preparations to entertain you suitably. Let me advise you, sir, to listen to my sister. Those who are not carried away, as you are, by the vehemence of their feelings, but can judge of things calmly, must see that you are getting too old, and therefore — but be guided by my sister's wisdom.

Lear: And this, you think, is a becoming speech on your part?

Regan: I swear it is, my lord. Do you not think that fifty knights form a sufficient train? What necessity can there be for a large number, or even for so many? Considerations both of expense and risk would seem to favor a still smaller band. How are two large companies of people, serving different masters, to be expected to dwell together in friendship under the same roof? It will be difficult; indeed, almost impracticable.

Goneril: Might we not arrange that the servants of each household, my sister's and my own, should wait upon you, my lord, while you are with us?

Regan: What reason could there be against it? It would be a much better arrangement, for in that case, if any of them failed in their duty, or in respect towards you, we should be able to rebuke them and enforce our wishes. When you come to my house, I must beg you to let only five and twenty accompany you. I see the risk of receiving more and I shall refuse admittance to any larger number.

Lear: For you I deprived myself of everything.

Regan: And it was time you did so!

Lear: Gave you charge even of myself, bequeathed you all I had and kept nothing back — nothing, but this one thing: the one condition I made was that I should retain a hundred knights for my own service. Is it five and twenty you say, Regan, that you will allow me?

Regan: I said so and will repeat it. I will have no larger number.

Lear: An evil person seems a little less evil when we find others who are worse. It is at least one degree upward to be not quite so wicked as another. *[To Goneril.]* I will come to your house. You allowed me fifty knights, which is twice the number Regan is willing to allow me. Therefore, your love is evidently double hers.

Goneril: Listen to me, sir, a moment. I do not see the necessity for twenty-five, or ten, or half as many, to be of your train, in a dwelling where there are many times that number ready to wait upon you and ordered to do you service.

Regan: What need is there even for one?

Lear: O, the necessity is not the point in question! If we are to have only necessities, then the poorest creature on earth has something which is not absolutely needful. If we are to confine ourselves to mere necessities, then human beings need only live as do the beasts of the field. You, a woman, do not actually need the fine garments with which you are clothed. Nature only demands sufficient clothing to keep life in you; the rest is superfluous. There is no necessity for fine garments, yet you wear them. What one's real need may be — O ye gods, grant me my present need — patience. Help me to endure! Behold me, O heavenly powers, an aged man before you, with a weight of sorrow as heavy as my weight of years, overwhelmed with the misery alike of distress and age! If it be your will that I suffer all this at my daughters' hands, at least strengthen me to bear it like a man and enable my righteous anger to keep me from weak tears, the refuge of women. No, you inhuman creatures, I will not weep. I will take vengeance upon you — such vengeance as shall — I know not yet what I will do, but the whole world shall be shocked when they hear of it! You think your cruelty will drive me to tears? Never! though with good reason might I weep. But rather than humble myself to tears before you, my heart will burst with its load of grief and shatter itself to fragments. O fool, my senses will leave me!

[Exeunt Lear, Gloucester, Kent and fool.
Storm and tempest.]

Cornwall: We had better retire. A tempest is rising.

Regan: There is scarcely room for the aged king and his attendants in this small dwelling.

Goneril: The fault lies with himself. He has left a comfortable home and must take the consequences of his foolishness.

Regan: I would welcome him personally with pleasure, but not his crowd of attendants.

Goneril: I have resolved on the same course. Where has the Earl of Gloucester gone?

Cornwall: Out after the aged Lear. Here he comes back again.

Gloucester: The king is terribly angry.

Cornwall: Where does he intend to go?

Gloucester: I do not know, but he has ordered his people to mount.

Cornwall: It is better to let him do as he will. He will go his own way.

Goneril: Do not think of begging him to remain.

Gloucester: Alas! night has almost fallen, and the tempest is rising. The chill winds are blowing keenly, and there is no shelter for miles around.

Regan: My dear lord, when people are obstinate and wilful, then we must leave their own bitter experiences, which they bring upon themselves, to teach them a lesson. Close your gates against them, for his lawless followers may very easily gain his ear, as he is so liable to give heed to their tales, and prudence would advise you to guard against any attack they may instigate him to make.

Cornwall: Take my wife's advice, my lord, and close the doors of your dwelling. Come inside and take shelter from the rising tempest.

[Exeunt.]

46

ACT III • SCENE 1

[A heath.]

[Storm still. Enter Kent and a gentleman, meeting.]

Kent: Who comes, except the storm?

Gentleman: One whose thoughts are as troubled as the night.

Kent: I recognize you. Where is King Lear?

Gentleman: Out struggling with the raging storm and crying to the howling gale to blow the solid land into the ocean or drive the foaming waves higher and higher, till they overwhelm the land, so that, in either case, the existing dreadful state of things may end; plucking at his hoary locks, which the fierce winds blow against heedlessly in their blind rage; and trying with puny human strength to out-do the striving of the elements and disdain their fury. Bareheaded, he goes through the storm, on such a night as this, when the bear, rather than face the howling winds, might resist the cry of her cubs, refusing to go forth in search of food. Even the lion and hungry wolf would seek shelter from such a tempest.

Kent: Is he alone?

Gentleman: Only his jester is with him, trying to divert his thoughts from the keen wounds his heart has received.

Kent: I have noticed you, sir, and have observed that you are a man to be trusted. Relying on the truth of my observations, I am not afraid to confide to you a very important matter. The king's two sons-in-law are at enmity with each other, although as yet it is secret enmity, cunningly concealed on the part of each duke. In the service of each, there are men, such as are to be found in the train of everyone of exalted rank, who appear as retainers of theirs, but who are, at the same time, scouts and watchers on behalf of the King of France, reporting to him the state of our kingdom and the events which occur here.

They have reported all that is known, both of the secret quarrels, plots and intrigues of the two dukes and the cruel treatment shown to the good old king. Whether from these causes or not, I cannot tell, or whether there is a further reason, of which these are but the outward signs, the fact remains that a French force is ready to invade this disunited country. Indeed, they have already taken advantage of our carelessness and secretly gathered strength in some of the most important seaports, in readiness to raise their standard openly. Now, this is what I wish you to do: hurry to Dover, if you can place belief in what I say to you, and there you will meet with those who will be grateful to you for the news you bring. To them you must relate the truth concerning the cruel treatment of the aged king and tell what just cause he has to complain of the inhuman behavior of those who are fast driving him out of his wits. I am of good family and know of what I am speaking and, having this certainty, I give you the opportunity of doing this service.

Gentleman: We will speak of this again later.

Kent: There is no time for delay. In proof that my real circumstances are far above those which my outward appearance would seem to convey, look within this purse and take its contents for your own. If you find, at Dover, the king's youngest daughter, as you undoubtedly will, let her see this ring, and she will then let you know what, at present, is unknown to you, the real name and rank of your present companion. A plague upon this terrible weather! I will go and look for the old king.

Gentleman: Your hand upon the bargain. Have you now said all you wish to tell me?

Kent: There is just one thing more, but it is more important than anything else at present. We must find Lear at once. You search diligently in that direction, and I will take this one, and the one who first discovers him must shout to let the other know.

[Exeunt severally.]

ACT III • SCENE 2

[Another part of the heath. Storm still.]
[Enter Lear and fool.]

Lear: Rage, wild blasts, till you burst your swollen cheeks! Shriek and rave, ye howling winds! Pour down, ye torrents of rain and ye water-spouts; gush forth till the vanes above the towers are overwhelmed in the rush of waters! You flashing lightning-flames, swifter than thought, heralds of the splitting thunder-stroke, fall on my gray hairs. And you, rolling thunders that make the whole earth tremble, crush the round globe into flatness! Grind it together into a shapeless mass, till every seed of life is crushed, and nothing is left that can prolong the race of ungrateful humanity!

Fool: Good master, a dry dwelling is better than this drenching in the open air, even at the cost of fair words and flattery. Go indoors, good uncle, and beg your daughter to give you shelter. A night like this takes no account of rights and wrongs, nor considers either man's folly or wisdom.

Lear: Roll and roar your fill, re-echoing thunder! Pour down in torrents, rain, and flash, you lightnings! None of you are my children. I will not call you cruel. I never owned you as sons or daughters. You never owed me obedience or submission, nor did I ever give my all to you! Work your will upon me! I am here, exposed to all your fury, an aged, feeble man, scorned and powerless. Yet I tell you, you are slavish servants, leagued with a pair of wicked daughters, and uniting your mighty forces in cruelty with theirs, all making war against an aged, gray-haired man. Oh! it is monstrous!

Fool: The man has a useful head-covering who has a roof over himself on a night like this. The man who has mistaken his feet for his heart and spent all his care upon them instead of the more vital organ is likely to be troubled when corns appear and to lose much sleep with the pain which he has courted. Well, every pretty maid at some time makes faces in her mirror!

Lear: No, I will not speak. I will endure without complaining.

[Enter Kent.]

Kent: Who is that?

Fool: Indeed, here is folly and wisdom both together.

Kent: Oh, my lord, are you out in this storm, when even the birds and beasts, which love to roam abroad in the darkness, have crept to shelter? The angry heavens have terrified them, so that they remain in their dens and caverns. In all my life, I have never known such terrible lightnings, such awful thunder-rolls or such a howling, roaring tempest. The pain and terror of it are more than human beings can endure.

Lear: Now the mighty powers of heaven, who are causing all this tumult in the skies, may discover and expose their foes. Quake, miserable man, who art conscious of many evil deeds, which have never received their punishment at the hands of earthly justice, and let the murderer fly to conceal himself, whose hands are steeped in blood! Hide, hypocrite, your evil passions from the light of day, and you who have falsely sworn! Tremble, cowards, who with outward kindliness and false friendship have treacherously plotted against the life of others! All ye hidden sins, burst your restraining bonds and come forth. See if you may hope to sue for mercy when these awful calls are sounding. My own misfortunes are the result of others' faults, rather than my own.

Kent: Alas! He has not even a covering for his head! My worthy master, here is a little hut near at hand. The owners will surely have kindness enough to give you shelter from the storm within it. Rest there awhile, and I will go back to that dwelling, where the inmates' hearts are more stony than the walls, and compel them to extend their grudging hospitality to you, even though they have just refused me entrance when I enquired for you, my lord.

Lear: I think I am beginning to lose my senses! Come along, fool. How are you, my lad? Do you feel cold? I do. Take us to the shelter you speak of, my good man, and show us the straw to rest on. Necessity has the curious quality of making worthless things seem of much value. Let us seek this hut. My poor jester, my faithful lad, there is yet a corner in my heart that grieves for your misfortunes.

Fool: *[Singing.]* The man who has but small wisdom (with hey, ho, the wind and the rain!) must not complain about his lot in life, for down come the showers every day!

Lear: You are right, my lad. Come, show us the way to the hut.

Fool: Let me foretell the future a little before I follow them. When the clergy think more of religion than of material things, when water is used to spoil good ale, when tailors are taught by men of rank, when lovers are put to death, but heretics allowed to go free, when no unfair judgment is given in law, when every squire and knight has money enough, when no one ever slanders another, when thieves cease to be found in a crowd, then shall this land come to disorder and destruction, and those who are living then will find that the best use to make of their feet is to flee with them. This prediction shall be accounted one of Merlin's when he comes after me.

[Exit.]

ACT III • SCENE 3

[Gloucester's castle.]
[Enter Gloucester and Edmund.]

Gloucester: Alas! my son, this treatment of the old king seems to me inhuman. His son and daughter have refused to allow me to exercise any authority in my own house because I begged them to let me befriend him. They said I should never be forgiven if, in spite of their commands, I attempted either to intercede for him or to relieve him in any way.

Edmund: How excessively cruel and inhuman!

Gloucester: Never mind. Do not show your displeasure. The Dukes of Cornwall and Albany are at enmity with each other, and a letter has come to me tonight, giving me news of even greater importance. I have put it securely away in my chamber, for it is not safe to have such news talked about, but the king's cruel wrongs will soon be fully avenged. A large contingent of troops has already landed. We must take Lear's side.

I shall go out now and look for him and secretly relieve his needs. You must remain in the duke's company and engage him in conversation so that he will not notice my absence. You can say I am not well and have retired to my room, if he should enquire for me. I must assist the aged king, even if my life is to pay the penalty, as indeed that is the risk I run. We shall see surprising events soon, my son. Let me beg you to be wise.

[Exit.]

Edmund: I shall tell Cornwall at once of your kindness to the old king, which he forbade you to show, and shall tell him the news you have received also. I think he will judge that I deserve much for this. Indeed, I may expect to gain by it all that Gloucester will forfeit, and that will be the whole of his possessions. Youth shall prosper on the downfall of old age.

[Exit.]

ACT III · SCENE 4

[The heath. Before a hovel.]
[Enter Lear, Kent and fool.]

Kent: This is the hut, sir. My worthy master, come inside. Poor human beings are unable to withstand the tempest raging out of doors.

[Storm still.]

Lear: Do not pester me further.

Kent: Come within the hut, dear master.

Lear: You tear my bosom with your pleading!

Kent: I would tear my own first. Worthy sir, come within.

Lear: It seems a terrible thing to you that this raging tempest drenches us through, but we do not feel these lesser ills so acutely when we are overwhelmed by worse evils. If you met a bear, you would naturally flee from it. But if the only way of escape was barred by the stormy ocean, you would think little of the danger to be feared from the bear and would meet it face to face.

It is only when we are free from mental troubles that we are so anxious about bodily comforts. But my poor mind is so torn by distracting thoughts that I have ceased to feel my body's discomfort. I am conscious of nothing but the sorrows throbbing in my bosom. That a child should be so ungrateful to a parent! As justly might the teeth wound the fingers that put food into the mouth! My vengeance shall strike deep! I will not be overcome. They shall not have power to move me to tears agin. To refuse me shelter on such a night! But I will endure the storm and the drenching rain! O my daughters, to shut out your loving old father, who so freely let you have everything he possessed. Oh! let me not think of it. Let me forget, lest my mind give way entirely; let me forget!

Kent: Dear master, come within.

Lear: Enter yourself, I beg. Seek shelter and more comfortable quarters. As for me, the raging of the storm will keep my mind from thoughts which would wound more keenly than the lightning-flashes. Well, I will enter. *[To the fool.]* Go in, my lad, before me. O homeless poor — no, do not wait for me. I will say a prayer first and rest afterwards. *[Fool goes in.]* Without covering from the storm, hungry and scantily clothed, exposed to the fury of such merciless weather, how can your pitiful rags afford you protection from such tempests? And how can your ill-nourished frames endure it, without a roof to shelter them? I have not thought sufficiently of the poor! If those of high rank and wealth were to experience but once what is endured by these poor unfortunate creatures, it would be a wholesome medicine for their pride, and would move them to bestow some of their superfluous wealth on these miserable ones, distributing more equally the gifts of the gods.

Edgar: *[Within.]* Fathom and half, fathom and half! Poor Tom!

[Fool runs out from the hovel.]

Fool: Help! Help! Do not go in there, good uncle. A ghost is inside!

Kent: Take hold of my hand. Who is it?

Fool: A spirit who calls himself poor Tom!

Kent: Who are you, there, muttering to yourself among the straw? Come out and show yourself!

[Enter Edgar, disguised as a madman.]

Edgar: Begone! I am haunted by an evil spirit. The chill blast is blowing through the frozen may-trees. Go home and be warm in your cold bed!

Lear: Did you give everything to your two daughters? Is it that which has brought you to such wretchedness?

Edgar: Who will bestow his charity on poor Tom? The evil spirit haunts him and leads him through fire and through water, over marshes and swamps, and lays knives and ropes in his way to tempt him to end his life. It tries to poison him, too, and leads him on mad wild-goose chases after his own shadow. Blessings be upon all your five senses! Tom feels chilly. Oh! dear, dear, dear. May you be preserved from all tempests, infections and star-blight! Bestow your charity on poor Tom, who is tormented by an evil spirit. There, he is beginning to worry me again!

[Storm still.]

Lear: Is it his daughters who have brought him to such misery? Did you give them everything? Could you keep nothing for yourself?

Fool: Oh! he saved a blanket to cover his nakedness.

Lear: May all the ills which are ever ready to fall in vengeance upon man fall upon those daughters of yours!

Kent: He has none, my lord.

Lear: How dare you say so, villain! Nothing but ungrateful daughters could have brought a human being to such depths! It seems to be the custom that the fathers who have been thus cast off should expose and wound their bodies in this way. It is a righteous retribution. It was the body which brought forth those daughters, who are prospering on the very life-blood of their parents.

Edgar: Pillicock sat on Pillicock hill; aha, aha, aha!

Fool: We shall all lose our wits soon in this cold.

Edgar: Beware of the evil spirit; disobey not your father and mother; never break a promise; have a care of your words; do not covet your neighbor's wife; and desire not riches and fine living. Tom feels chilly.

Lear: What were you formerly?

Edgar: A vain and haughty servant, a swaggering jack-a-dandy, that wore women's favors in my cap and made vows and protestations with every breath, only to break them unblushingly, that never wearied in planning wickedness and that loved women, drink and gambling; one whose heart was faithless, whose ear was ready for eavesdropping and whose hand was quick to strike, who was lazy as a hog, cunning as a fox, ravenous as a wolf, fierce as a mad dog and savage as a lion. Never let a woman's arts move thee and beware of the evil spirit! The chilly blast is still blowing through the may-trees, whistling as it goes. Stand still, my lad, while it passes.

[Storm still.]

Lear: It would be better for you to be sheltered in the tomb, rather than be exposed thus naked to the storm. Is this all that a man is, without the addition of trappings and ornament? Regard him carefully. He has taken no silk from the worm, nor leather from the beast; the sheep has not provided him with wool, nor the civet cat with scent. Here are three in this company who are artificial — he is the natural, genuine article. Humanity, unfurnished and unadorned, is merely a miserable two-legged thing like that! Away with these externals! Loosen these trappings!

[Tearing off his clothes.]

Fool: Don't be dissatisfied, I beg of you, uncle. It is a rough night to take the water. See, here comes a flame towards us!

[Enter Gloucester, with a torch.]

Edgar: Here comes the goblin Flibbertigibbet. He comes out when the curfew bell rings and roams about till dawn. It is he that strikes people with blindness and disfigures their faces, blasts the corn and is cruel to the helpless beasts of the field. St. Withold three times walked the world and met the evil creatures of night, whom he checked and made to pledge their word, and— begone, witch, away!

Kent: How is your highness?

Lear: Who is that?

Kent: What do you want, sir? Who are you?

Gloucester: Who are you in here? What are you called?

Edgar: I am poor Tom that feeds on frogs and toads and foul things that live in the water and that he finds on the land and whose drink is the scum of the stagnant water; who is flogged from one parish to another and put in the stocks and in jail; but who once had plenty to eat, plenty to wear and who rode on horseback with a sword at his side. But for many a year poor Tom has lived on such creatures as mice and rats. Take care! the foul fiend is still worrying me! Keep still, Smulkin; be quiet, thou evil spirit!

Gloucester: Is this the company I find your highness in?

Edgar: You need not say anything against his manners. He is sometimes known as Modo and sometimes as Mahu.

Gloucester: Your grace, our children have fallen so low as to turn against their own parents — my children as well as yours!

Edgar: Poor Tom feels chilly.

Gloucester: Come back with me to my house, my lord. I cannot allow your daughters' cruel orders to compel me against my will to leave you here. They commanded me to shut you out from my house and leave you to the mercy of this cruel weather, but I have come, nevertheless, to find you and take you back to where shelter and warmth are awaiting you.

Lear: Let me first have a little conversation with this wise man. How is thunder caused?

Kent: My dear lord, accept his kindness and go home with him.

Lear: I will speak first with this wise Egyptian. What subjects do you devote yourself to?

Edgar: Chiefly to keeping away evil spirits and to killing evil beasts.

Lear: I should like to ask you one question when we are alone.

Kent: Ask him again to come with you, sir. His mind is beginning to wander.

Gloucester: Can you wonder at it? *[Storm still.]* His own children have turned against him and wish him to live no longer. Ah, the faithful Kent, who was so unkindly banished, foretold that this would happen. You tell me the king's mind is beginning to wander. I can say truly that my own mind is in danger of doing likewise. My own son, whom I have now disowned, only recently plotted against me and would have slain me. Never did a parent love a child more dearly than I loved my son. In truth, sorrow has nearly driven me mad. What a terrible storm! I beg your highness . . .

Lear: Pardon me, sir. Most learned man, let me have your society.

Edgar: How cold poor Tom feels!

Gloucester: Go within the hut, sir; shelter inside.

Lear: Let us all go in together.

Kent: Come with us, sir.

Lear: I will come with him. I will stay beside the learned doctor.

Kent: Let us humor him, my lord, and let the man come with us.

Gloucester: Bring him with you.

Kent: Come along, fellow, and accompany us.

Lear: Yes, come, my wise Grecian.

Gloucester: Now do not speak; be silent all!

Edgar: Child Rowland approached the gloomy tower, saying — Ha, ha, ha! My nose tells me that an Englishman is near.

[Exeunt.]

ACT III • SCENE 5

[Gloucester's castle.]
[Enter Cornwall and Edmund.]

Cornwall: I will not leave here till he is punished for this.

Edmund: I am somewhat afraid to think how my conduct will appear, since my loyalty to you overcomes my loyalty to my father.

Cornwall: I can see plainly now that Edgar's own wickedness was not the only thing which led him to attempt your father's life, but that your father's own ill-doings may have helped to urge him on.

Edmund: I am most unfortunately placed, for I am in a position when doing right brings sorrow on myself. Here is the letter to which he referred and which proves that he knows of France's movements. Oh! that it had not been my fate to discover this, or that such treachery had not existed!

Cornwall: Come with me to my wife.

Edmund: You will have important matters to consider, if the news in this letter be true.

Cornwall: Whether true or not, the result is the same so far as you are concerned. You are now the Earl of Gloucester.

Edmund: *[Aside.]* It would make him more certain still of my father's treachery, if I find that my father has been giving aid to the king. I will never fail in my duty to you, my lord, though it will be a severe struggle to overcome my natural feelings of affection.

Cornwall: I will load you with honors and responsibility, and my affection shall more than supply your father's place.

[Exeunt.]

ACT III • SCENE 6

[A chamber in a farmhouse adjoining the castle.]
[Enter Gloucester, Lear, Kent, fool and Edgar.]

Gloucester: You will be more comfortable here than outside in the storm. I am glad to be able to do even so little for you, and you must be grateful. I will bring anything else I can obtain, to add to your comfort, and will return as quickly as possible.

Kent: May the heavenly powers repay you, sir, for your goodness to him. His mind is greatly weakened by grief and resentment.

[Exit Gloucester.]

Edgar: I hear Frateretto's voice telling me that Nero is now passing his time fishing in the infernal lake. Say your prayers, my poor fellow, and avoid the evil spirit.

Fool: Tell me, sir, I pray, whether a man who has lost his wits is a gentleman or a yeoman.

Lear: Neither; it is only kings who lose their wits!

Fool: You are wrong. It is a yeoman whose son has been made a gentleman, for only a fool would set up his son to be better than himself.

Lear: They should be scourged with fire.

Edgar: The goblin is biting me!

Fool: None but those who are witless would place any faith in the gentleness of a beast of prey, the continued health of a steed or the lasting affection of a youth.

Lear: Yes, I will do it. They shall be brought to trial at once. *[To Edgar.]* Take this place, wise judge. *[To the fool.]* You, most learned sir, will take this seat. Now, vixens, we bring you before the court!

Edgar: See how fiercely he stares at them! Is it necessary for you to play the coquette, madam? Cross the stream, Bessie, and come to me.

Fool: Her boat is not safe, and she may not tell why she fears to come over to thee.

Edgar: The evil spirit sings like a nightingale. And another goblin in poor Tom's stomach is crying for food. Be quiet, goblin; I cannot feed thee!

Kent: How are you now, my lord? Come and rest here upon these pillows. Do not weary yourself with standing longer.

Lear: Wait until they have been tried. Let the witnesses come in. *[To Edgar.]* Take your appointed seat, worthy judge, in your robes. *[To the fool.]* And you, sir, his fellow-judge, seat yourself at his side. *[To Kent.]* You, too, belong to the court; be seated also.

Edgar: Let us judge fairly. Are you sleeping or do you waken, merry herdsman? Your flock has strayed among the wheat. They will never hear a call from that dainty little mouth! Purr, the cat is gray.

Lear: Place this one, Goneril, on trial first. I swear before this noble company that she actually assaulted her father, the king.

Fool: Stand forward, madam. Are you called Goneril?

Lear: She dare not say that she is not.

Fool: I beg your pardon, I thought you were a joint-stool.

Lear: And here is a second one. You may see by her distorted and twisted features the kind of feelings she harbors in her heart. Stop her! Do not let her escape! Flame and sword! Is there treachery here? Faithless judge, why did you not detain her?

Edgar: Blessings upon thy poor senses!

Kent: Dear master, you said you would be patient and endure. Have you forgotten it?

Edgar: *[Aside.]* My grief for the poor old king is beginning to overmaster me. I shall not be able to keep up this pretence of madness long.

Lear: Even the hounds that I knew all bark at me now!

Edgar: Tom will frighten them away for you. Every kind of mouth that can bite, every tooth, every breed of hound from a mastiff to a tiny spaniel, Tom will make them howl and run when he throws his head at them. Oh, dear, dear! Here, stop that, and let us be off to market-towns, to fairs and funeral feasts. Poor Tom has nothing to drink.

Lear: After that, let Regan be dissected and see what disease lies at her heart. Is there a natural reason for hearts so hard as theirs? *[To Edgar.]* I will take you, sir, to be one of my five-score attendants. But I dislike the style of your clothing. No doubt you will tell me they are cut in the Persian fashion, but I would rather you altered them.

Kent: My dear lord, lie down now and take some rest.

Lear: Quietly, quietly then. Pull the curtains round. There, there; we will have supper in the morning; there, there.

Fool: And I will go to sleep at midday.

[Re-enter Gloucester.]

Gloucester: Come near to me, my good man. Is the king, your master, still here?

Kent: Yes, my lord, but leave him in peace. He is no longer sane.

Gloucester: Carry him away quickly, kind fellow. I have discovered that his enemies are planning his death. I have provided a stretcher for him, and you must make all speed to Dover, where you will be welcomed joyfully and sheltered gladly. Take the old king in your arms, my friend, and convey him quickly from this place, without further loitering. In a very short space of time, it will be too late to save him, and all those who try to befriend him will also most assuredly forfeit their lives. Lift him up quickly. Follow me at once, and I will set you speedily on the road to safety.

Kent: Wearied nature is sunk in repose. This sweet slumber might have eased the poor king's overtaxed limbs and wearied brain. If the opportunity passes, it will be almost impossible for him to recover. *[To the fool.]* Come, aid me to carry your master; you must come with him.

Gloucester: Hurry, hurry!

[Exeunt all but Edgar.]

Edgar: When we behold those far above us in rank enduring the same hardships that we do ourselves, we are less inclined to cry out against fate. Those who are lonely in their sorrow suffer most. Their minds brood over what they have lost, but when we have companions in grief, suffering seems to be much lightened. How much more bearable my own trouble seems, now that I have seen the poor king overwhelmed with the same grief, he treated cruelly by his children, and I by my father. I must away now and not reveal myself till these lying tales, which wrong me so, are proved false and the proofs of my innocence cause me to be reconciled to my father and resume my place in his love. May the king escape safely. Let what will happen besides! Now hide! Hide!

[Exit.]

ACT III • SCENE 7

[Gloucester's castle.]

[Enter Cornwall, Regan, Goneril, Edmund and servants.]

Cornwall: Ride quickly to the Duke of Albany and let him see this letter. The French forces are already upon our shores. Look for that traitor, Gloucester.

[Exeunt some of the servants.]

Regan: Let him be hanged at once!

Goneril: Let him be blinded!

Cornwall: Leave his punishment to me. You, Edmund, had better accompany Goneril. It is not fitting that you should have to witness your father's punishment for his treachery. When you reach the Duke of Albany, counsel him to prepare as speedily as possible to meet these foes, and I will engage to do the same. We will keep each other advised of our proceedings by speedy and capable messengers. Adieu, dear Goneril. Adieu, my Lord of Gloucester!

[Enter Oswald.]

Well! have you found the king?

Oswald: The Earl of Gloucester has helped him away from

here. Several of the knights of his train, searching eagerly for him, met him just setting out; they joined forces with several of Gloucester's men and have taken him in the direction of Dover, triumphing in the fact that there they will meet friends able to protect him.

Cornwall: Get your lady's steeds ready.

Goneril: Adieu, my dear lord, and Regan.

Cornwall: Adieu, Edmund.

[Exeunt Goneril, Oswald and Edmund.]

Go and find the villain, Gloucester. Bring him here, bound like a robber.

[Exeunt other servants.]

Though I cannot sentence him to be put to death without any formal trial, yet my authority may stretch a little in this case, where there is such cause for anger, and, though men might condemn it they cannot forbid the exercise of it. Is that the treacherous villain?

[Enter Gloucester, brought in by two or three.]

Regan: That is the man, the artful wretch!

Cornwall: See that his withered old arms are firmly secured.

Gloucester: What can your highnesses mean by this? Remember I am your host. Good friends, do not harm me!

Cornwall: Pinion him fast, I tell you.

[Servants bind him.]

Regan: Tightly, tightly! O the foul villain!

Gloucester: I am no villain, you hard-hearted woman!

Cornwall: Fasten him to this seat. You shall learn, knave!

[Regan plucks his beard.]

Gloucester: Merciful heavens! It is a mean act to pull my white hairs.

Regan: To think that so aged a man is capable of such treachery!

Gloucester: Wicked woman, those gray hairs of which you have cruelly robbed me shall come to life and condemn your conduct. Remember that you are, at present, in my house, partaking of my hospitality. It is unwise to treat your host in this manner! Why do you do this?

Cornwall: Now, sir, tell us what news you have heard from France.

Regan: And do not try to deceive us, for we have found out all.

Cornwall: And how far are you in league with the rebels who have just landed on these shores?

Regan: To whose care have you committed the mad old Lear? Tell us!

Gloucester: All the news I have received is from one who is taking no part in the strife and whose information is the merest conjecture of what may happen.

Cornwall: Crafty!

Regan: And untrue!

Cornwall: Where did you give orders that Lear was to be taken?

Gloucester: To Dover.

Regan: Why should you choose Dover? Were you not forbidden . . .

Cornwall: Why choose Dover? Let us hear that first.

Gloucester: I am bound and helpless before my foes and must endure the baiting!

Regan: Why choose Dover, sir?

Gloucester: Because I hoped to save him from your cruelty, to save his poor old face from being torn by your wicked hands and his kingly person from destruction at the hands of the savage Goneril. Had such a storm raged on the ocean as poured down upon his uncovered head in the inky darkness, the billows would have reared themselves up to the skies and extinguished the lamps of heaven. But the tears of the poor, broken-hearted king mingled with the showers! If even the fiercest beasts of prey had whined at your doors for admittance on that pitiless night, you might have allowed them shelter, forgetting their natural cruelties in terror of the storm. But I shall live to behold swift retribution fall upon such daughters!

Cornwall: You shall never behold it. I will destroy those eyes, so that you shall see never more! Hold the seat, you men!

Gloucester: If there is anyone here who hopes to live long, help me! Aid me! O unmerciful! O heavens!

Regan: Destroy the other also! Make both sides alike!

Cornwall: If ever you behold retribution . . .

First Servant: Stop, my lord! No more! I have been in your service all my life, and, believe me, in all my years of service, I have never yet done you such a good turn as I do now when I ask you to cease from such work!

Regan: What do you mean, you cur?

First Servant: If you were a man, instead of a woman, I would strike you for your share in this!

Cornwall: My serf! How dare you!

[They draw their swords and fight.]

First Servant: Come on and take the consequences, if you will have it so.

Regan: A slave to defy his master! Let me have this sword!

[Takes a sword and runs at him from behind.]

First Servant: O, you have killed me! You can still, sir, use one of your eyes to see him hurt! Oh!

[Dies.]

Cornwall: I shall take sure means to prevent him seeing anything again. Now he has lost both! What light have you now?

Gloucester: None! All is gloom and misery! Where is my child? Edmund, my son, let every spark of natural affection burn within you to urge you to take vengeance for this hateful deed!

Regan: Faithless traitor! You are imploring aid from one who will never give it, for he has no love for you whatever. He was the friend who disclosed to us your treachery and he is too loyal himself to feel any sorrow at your fate!

Gloucester: Oh! I was mad to mistrust Edgar! He has been wronged. Pardon me, kind heaven, for that folly and bless and guard him.

Regan: Put him out of the castle and let him grope the road to his friends as best he may!

[Exit servant with Gloucester.]

What is it, my husband? How do you feel?

Cornwall: I have been sorely wounded. Come, let us go. Send that blind old knave about his business and fling that slave's body out of doors! My blood is flowing fast. Help me, Regan. This has happened at a most unfortunate time.

[Exit Cornwall, led by Regan.]

Second Servant: If vengeance does not fall upon that man, I, for one, will never more try to live well.

Third Servant: And if his wife does not meet a speedy death, but lives till age brings her to the grave, women, by her example, will soon become inhuman creatures!

Second Servant: We will go after the aged Gloucester and seek out mad Tom to be his guide. The witless fellow will readily agree, for it matters not to him what he does.

Third Servant: You seek them out, and I will bring something to heal his poor injured face. The gods be his aid!

[Exeunt severally.]

ACT IV · SCENE 1

[The heath.]
[Enter Edgar.]

Edgar: This lowly position of mine, of open wretchedness, is, after all, better than being doomed to misery and yet buoyed up by false hopes and plausible pretences. There is always hope, even for the most forlorn and wretched creature, for the lowest can get no lower. Any change of his state must be in the direction of a return to better things. The change to be bewailed is one from the happiest state, for then all change is for the worse, while the poor creature at the lowest ebb of misery may always live in hope, while he need fear nothing at all. I salute you, then, wild winds that strike me! Invisible breezes, to whom I stretch my arms in greeting, the poor creature you have worked your will upon is yet independent of your favors and can defy you! Who is this approaching?

[Enter Gloucester, led by an old man.]

My father, guided by a poor old man! O earth! How carelessly we might live on, love of life contending against the attacks of age, if the wild changes and uncertainties of fortune did not make us glad to leave you!

Old Man: I have lived on your land, my dear master, and on your father's before you for eighty years.

Gloucester: Leave me, my friend. Good fellow, go away. You cannot help me in the least and you may bring harm upon yourself by showing kindness to me.

Old Man: Alas, my lord, you are unable to find your way alone.

Gloucester: There is no particular way I wish to find. Therefore, it does not matter that I cannot see it. When I had the use of my eyes, I went wrong and did not walk securely. It often is so and, frequently, it happens that our very losses turn out to be our best securities. Ah! my dear son, your father was deceived, and you were the victim of the treachery! If I could only meet my beloved Edgar again and feel his hand clasping mine, I should rejoice as though I had received my sight.

Old Man: Hello! Who is that?

Edgar: *[Aside.]* Heavens! None surely can decide when he has reached the lowest depths of misery! I thought I had, but here is heavier sorrow.

Old Man: It is the poor, wandering Bedlamite.

Edgar: *[Aside.]* There may be worse to come. As long as we can speculate about our condition, we have not touched the lowest depths.

Old Man: Where are you going, my man?

Gloucester: Is he a beggar?

Old Man: Yes, and witless as well.

Gloucester: He cannot be quite insane, or he would not have sufficient wit to beg. I saw one who seemed to answer that description last night, in the tempest, and he seemed to me the most abject figure! Something turned my thoughts to my son Edgar then, though my thoughts of him were hard. But since then, I have learned much that I did not know at that moment. We poor mortals are the toys of fate. The gods crush and slay us for their pastime, as flies are crushed and tortured by heedless children!

Edgar: *[Aside.]* What can have happened? How unfortunate I am that, to keep up my disguise, I must jest in the face of grief! Blessings be on you, sir!

Gloucester: Is the mad creature speaking?

Old Man: Yes, my lord.

Gloucester: Go back, then, I beg you and bring some clothing for the poor fellow, if you will do such for the sake of the old affection you bear me. If you hasten, you will overtake us before we have travelled much farther on the way to Dover. I shall beg this poor fellow to guide me there.

Old Man: But, sir, alas! He is insane.

Gloucester: That is the general condition of affairs just now. Those who cannot see where they are going trust themselves to the leadership of those who are lacking in sense. However, do what I have told you, or do it not, as you please. But, in any case, leave me.

Old Man: He shall have the best clothes I possess, no matter what may be the consequence.

[Exit.]

Gloucester: Sir, naked fellow . . .

Edgar: Poor Tom feels chilly. *[Aside.]* I cannot pretend any longer!

Gloucester: Come near me, my man.

Edgar: *[Aside.]* But I must try awhile. Your poor eyes are hurt, master.

Gloucester: Do you know the road to Dover?

Edgar: Every road and pathway! Poor Tom has been sorely frightened. Preserve you, good sir, from the evil spirit. Five evil spirits have possessed poor Tom all at the same time: Obidicut, the sensual spirit; Hobbididence, the silent spirit; Mahu, the thieving spirit; Modo, the murdering spirit; and Flibbertigibbet, the grimacing spirit. He has since entered into chambermaids and servant maids. Therefore, may fortune smile upon you, kind sir!

Gloucester: Poor wretch, whom fate has hurt and the gods wounded with the strokes of misfortune, here is money for you. Your misery will appear less, now that another shares it. May it be so always, ye gods! May those who have a superabundance of life's good things, who take their fill of every desire, who, instead of obeying heaven's laws, make them subservient to their own pleasure, and who refuse to know that want and pain exist because they themselves are untouched by these things, may such as these be speedily touched by your influence and moved to share some of their surplus wealth with those in need, so that none may be left in want. Do you know the neighborhood of Dover?

Edgar: Yes, sir.

Gloucester: A lofty rock stands there, near to the shore, rearing its tall height above the ocean waves, over which it leans, as if gazing from that dread summit into the fearful depths. Guide me, I pray, only to the edge of that cliff, and I will amend your ill fortune by a gift of value. After that, I shall need a guide no more.

Edgar: Place your arm in mine. Poor Tom will be your guide.

[Exeunt.]

ACT IV • SCENE 2

[Before the Duke of Albany's palace.]
[Enter Goneril and Edmund.]

Goneril: Welcome to my house, Gloucester. It is marvellous that that meek spouse of mine has not come to meet us.

[Enter Oswald.]

Where is the Duke of Albany?

Oswald: He is here, in the palace, my lady. But he seems a different person. He only smiled when I informed him of the French invasion and, when I said you were on your way here, he replied, "So much the worse!" I gave him an account of the treason of which the Earl of Gloucester had been guilty and of the faithful services rendered by his son, Edmund, to Cornwall and his wife, and he said I was a fool, saying that I was looking at the wrong side of things. He seems to find satisfaction in the things which should give him most annoyance and vexation in what should please him most.

Goneril: *[To Edmund.]* In that case, your errand here is useless. You need not come in and see him. His cowardly heart will never undertake the enterprise. He will not acknowledge any injuries which would oblige him to resent them. The wishes we spoke of on our way here may be realized. Return to the Duke of Cornwall and help him to get his troops together quickly. You shall lead them, while I here try to take my husband's place, leaving him to womanish inaction. The faithful Oswald shall be our messenger, and, if you are bold enough to make a bid for fortune, you may soon receive a message from one who will command you as her own. Wear this favor. No — no words of thanks *[Giving a favor.]* but stoop down to me. If this kiss had a tongue, it could say words to you that would exalt your hopes to the skies! Understand me and adieu!

Edmund: My life is yours!

Goneril: Beloved Edmund.

[Exit Edmund.]

O how dissimilar one man and another may be! You are worthy, Edmund, of all that a woman may do to serve you. I am still bound, however, to my contemptible husband.

Oswald: Here is the duke, my lady.

[Exit.]
[Enter Albany.]

Goneril: I am of some value, you see!

Albany: O woman, you are less than the dust which is blown about by the rough gale! Your nature fills me with fear. Those who despise and ill-treat the very source of their own life, as you have done, can never be trusted again, nor can anyone say with certainty within what limits they may be restricted, or whether their savage nature will not break loose from all restraint again. One who severs herself so completely from the parent stem cannot but become a diseased creature, withering to decay!

Goneril: That is enough! The subject is ridiculous!

Albany: Yes, to the worthless all truth and virtue seems worthless. An evil mind has no taste for anything but evil. Wicked, savage creatures, what have you done! Driven out of his senses your own parent, a kind old father, whose gray hairs even a half-tamed bear would have respected. Inhuman creatures, lost to all sense of gratitude of filial love! How could Cornwall's manhood, his nobility, his gratitude for favors received, allow him to see it done! The human race will speedily descend to the level of the brutes, tearing each other apart with savage cruelty, unless the gods interpose to punish such wickedness and openly send down vengeance for such hideous wrong.

Goneril: Timid creature, who would wait for the stroke of insult and who would calmly endure any injuries heaped upon your head! You see not when to strike for your own advantage, or when to endure patiently, and you do not seem to understand that it is foolish to waste sympathy on a knave whom vengeance has overtaken before he has had time to complete his villainy. Why are you not sounding the alarm to your forces? The French troops are waving their flags gaily in our country, where no sound is heard of arms raised to resist them, and their knights advance to menace our position and rule, while you remain idly philosophizing and wondering why these things occur!

Albany: Look at yourself, fiendish woman! See your own wickedness before condemning others! A monstrous, inhuman disposition is more hideous in a woman than in the devil himself, for it is his own nature.

Goneril: Witless creature!

Albany: Perverted being, concealing a devilish nature under a woman's shape. For very shame, do not show your evil self so plainly! These hands of mine could tear you limb from limb, if I allowed the hot passion of my rage to overmaster me, but I will not stoop to so unseemly an act. You have a woman's form, and that protects you, notwithstanding the devilishness of your deeds.

Goneril: Restrain yourself, sir!

[Enter a messenger.]

Albany: What tidings do you bring?

Messenger: Oh, sir! The Duke of Cornwall has been killed! He was in the act of destroying the Earl of Gloucester's second eye when one of his servants slew him.

Albany: Destroying Gloucester's eyes!

Messenger: One of his own serfs was so moved with pity that he strove to prevent the horrid deed and turned his weapon against the powerful duke, whose anger was so fierce that, then and there, he struck him down in the midst of those standing around. He himself, however, had received so severe a wound that he has since died from it.

Albany: The gods still reign! This swift and righteous vengeance proves that still the heavenly judges execute justice and repay the wickedness of this lower world. But, O poor Gloucester! Was his other eye destroyed!

Messenger: Both, both, my lord! Lady, I bring you this letter from your sister who desires a reply immediately.

Goneril: *[Aside.]* From one point of view, the death of Cornwall is very satisfactory, but there is this disadvantage: that now Regan is free, and my beloved Edmund has gone back there. These things are likely to shatter all my dreams and bring my airy castles to the ground, leaving me wretched. If it were not for this, the tidings are agreeable enough. I will see what the letter says and give you the reply.

[Exit.]

Albany: Where was Edmund when his father was being so ill-treated?

Messenger: Travelling here with my mistress.

Albany: He is not here.

Messenger: No, sir. I met him returning.

Albany: Does he know of this terrible wrong?

Messenger: Yes, sir, he knows. He betrayed his father into Cornwall's hands and then intentionally left home, so that there might be no one in a position to hinder their vengeance.

Albany: From henceforth, Gloucester, my life shall be devoted to the task of avenging this cruel deed and of repaying your kindness to the poor old king. Come with me, my good fellow, and let me hear all you have to tell.

[Exeunt.]

ACT IV • SCENE 3

[The French camp near Dover.]
[Enter Kent and a gentleman.]

Kent: Can you tell me why the King of France has returned to his own country so unexpectedly?

Gentleman: A matter of state has recalled him, which he remembered had not been settled when he left the country. It was a matter which greatly endangered the welfare of France, and so important that his presence there was absolutely necessary.

Kent: Who is left in command during his absence?

Gentleman: The Marshal of France, Monsieur La Far.

Kent: Did the queen show any sorrow when she read your news?

Gentleman: Yes, indeed, sir. She read the letters while I was still with her, and, time after time, her beautiful face was wet with tears. But she controlled herself and remained mistress of her emotion, which, like a rebel, tried to conquer her.

Kent: Then she was affected by it?

Gentleman: Yes, but not to any passionate outburst. Grief and resignation vied with each other in her face, like sunshine and showers striving together. Her face was sweeter than an April day. The tiny, rippling smiles on her rosy mouth were heedless of the watery visitants in her eyes — dewy drops which fell like pearly showers from sparkling diamonds. Indeed, we should all fall in love with grief, if everyone in grieving looked so lovely.

Kent: Did she say nothing?

Gentleman: In truth, she now and then gasped, "Father," with a choking cry, as though there were a weight upon her heart. Then she cried, "Sisters! Sisters! O, disgrace to womanhood! Kent! Father! Sisters! What! Out in the tempest! In the darkness! Surely such a piteous tale could never be credited!" Then she let fall from her sweet eyes the sacred drops of pity that bathed her face while she made outcry of her grief. Then she hurriedly departed to weep in solitude.

Kent: It is fate! The planets rule our destinies and decree what we shall be. If it were not so, how could it be possible that the selfsame parents should have children of such opposite natures? Have you spoken with the queen again?

Gentleman: I have not.

Kent: Did this occur before the king had departed?

Gentleman: No, afterwards.

Kent: Well, sir, her poor, cheerless father is now in Dover. Occasionally, in his brighter moments, he remembers why we are here and then he is firm in his refusal to see Cordelia.

Gentleman: What is his reason, good sir?

Kent: He is overwhelmed by shame. He remembers that he treated her most cruelly, that he let her go to her marriage and to all the risks of foreign lands without his blessing and that he bestowed her just and rightful portion on those beastly sisters of hers. The recollection of all this cuts him so deeply that the intense humiliation he feels keeps him from going near her.

Gentleman: Alas! Poor Lear!

Kent: Have you no news of the forces of the two dukes?

Gentleman: Yes, we hear they are on the march.

Kent: Well, good sir, I will take you to where the king is staying and commit him to your charge. For the present, I am desirous of remaining unknown for a very urgent reason. You will not regret having given me your friendship when I reveal myself truly. Come with me, I beg.

[Exeunt.]

ACT IV • SCENE 4

[The same. A tent.]

[Enter, with drum and colors, Cordelia, doctor, and soldiers.]

Cordelia: Alas! It is my poor father. He has just been seen, as mad as the turbulent ocean. He was lifting up his voice in song and had decked himself with all the weeds and wild flowers that are to be found among the wheat fields. Take a hundred men and overlook not an inch of the ground, overgrown with the tall grass and corn. Search till he be found and fetch him here.

[Exit an officer.]

What can human knowledge do to bring back his lost reason? I will give all my wealth to the man who can restore him.

Doctor: It can be done, lady. There are means that can be

employed, the chief of which is Nature's own remedy —
rest. He greatly needs this, and there are many medicinal
herbs which will produce this effect and give to the suffering one a peaceful sleep.

Cordelia: May all the hidden virtues and healing herbs that
earth brings forth be watered by my tears and spring up to
help in the restoration of my dear father! Search for him
quickly, in case, in his wayward passion, he may end his life
for lack of the necessary guidance to preserve it.

[Enter a messenger.]

Messenger: I bring tidings, lady. The British troops are advancing towards this place.

Cordelia: We have already heard of it, and our forces are ready.
It is for your sake, my beloved parent, that this enterprise
has been undertaken. My powerful husband had compassion for me and yielded to my tears and prayers. We are
urged by no swelling desires of conquest and power, but
solely by the fond affection I bear to my father and a deter-
mination to restore him to his rights. May he quickly be
found and brought to me!

[Exeunt.]

ACT IV • SCENE 5

[Gloucester's castle.]
[Enter Regan and Oswald.]

Regan: Have the Duke of Albany's men taken the field?

Oswald: Yes, my lady.

Regan: Has he accompanied them?

Oswald: He has, though most unwillingly. His wife is more
eager for the fight than he.

Regan: Edmund of Gloucester did not see Albany when he
journeyed there, I understand.

Oswald: He did not, lady.

Regan: What is your mistress' letter to Edmund about?

Oswald: I cannot tell, madam.

Regan: He has ridden hurriedly away on an important errand. It
was a great mistake not to put the old earl to death after he
was blinded. Now, wherever he goes, he will be pitied, and
we shall be blamed. I believe Lord Edmund, out of compassion for his father's pitiful condition, has gone intending
to put an end to his darkened existence. At the same time,

73

he is to spy out the powers of the invaders.

Oswald: Then I must follow him, my lady, and deliver the letter.

Regan: My forces march tomorrow. You had better remain till then and ride with them, for travelling is not safe at present.

Oswald: That is impossible, lady. My mistress ordered me to carry out her wishes in this matter.

Regan: Why was it necessary to write at all? Why could you not have delivered her message verbally? Perhaps — it might be, I cannot tell — I will be your friend forever if you let me open the letter.

Oswald: My lady, I would sooner . . .

Regan: Your mistress has no affection for the Duke of Albany. I know that with certainty. On her recent visit to us here, she cast many loving looks and eloquent glances at Lord Edmund. You, I know, are in her confidence.

Oswald: I, madam?

Regan: I know what I am talking about. It is true. Let me counsel you to give your attention to this. My husband is now dead, and I am free. It is much more suitable that I should take Lord Edmund than that your mistress should think of it. He and I have already spoken about it. There is more which you may hear. When you meet Edmund, give him this and, when you tell your lady of all this, beg her not to give way to unwise anger, but to act with discretion. Adieu. If it should happen that you hear news of that treacherous Gloucester, let it be known that anyone who brings about his death will be well rewarded.

Oswald: I hope I may find him myself, my lady, and it would be seen on whose side I am.

Regan: Farewell.

[Exeunt.]

ACT IV · SCENE 6

[Fields near Dover.]
[Enter Gloucester and Edgar, dressed like a peasant.]

Gloucester: When shall we reach the summit of that cliff I told you of?

Edgar: You are going up the slope towards it now. Do you not feel what an effort it is?

Gloucester: We appear to me to be walking on level ground.

Edgar: On a terribly steep hill. Listen! Do you hear the sound of the waves?

Gloucester: Indeed, I cannot.

Edgar: I think your other faculties have lost their keenness from the injury to your sight.

Gloucester: Perhaps that is the case. Your voice sounds differently in my ears; your manner of speech, too, seems greatly improved.

Edgar: You are quite mistaken. I am still the same in every way, with the exception of my clothes.

Gloucester: Your speech appears to me much improved.

Edgar: Come along, sir, we have reached the place at last. Now, do not move. It is awful even to gaze from this giddy height down to the beach below! The birds flying to and fro half-way down look scarcely the size of beetles. Midway down the face of the cliff, a samphire-gatherer clings to the rock, engaged in his perilous calling. At that distance, he appears no larger than a man's head. The boatmen walking far below us on the shore are diminished by the distance to the size of mice. The lofty-masted vessel moored in the bay has shrunk till she seems no bigger than her own cock-boat, while the cock-boat itself appears but a tiny speck, scarcely visible upon the waters. The sound of the rolling waves, as they plunge upon the shingly beach, is inaudible from such a height as this. I must gaze no longer, or my head will swim, and my eyesight fail and I should fall and be dashed to pieces far below.

Gloucester: Place me on the spot where you are.

Edgar: Let me take your hand. Now you stand but a few inches from the very edge of the cliff. I would not spring up on that spot for all the wealth of the universe!

Gloucester: Now loosen your hold. Take this second purse from me, my good fellow. It contains a gem of much value. May all good spirits give you good fortune with it! Now leave me. Say farewell; I wish to hear you departing.

Edgar: Adieu, good sir.

Gloucester: Amen!

Edgar: My deception of him in his sorrow is only that I may find a remedy for his grief.

Gloucester: *[Kneeling.]* O heavenly powers! Here do I forsake the world and say farewell to life. Here before you, with resignation, do I cast away my sorrows and my misery. Could I have endured them longer, without rebelling against your resistless decrees, the last feeble flickerings of my wretched life should have died away, unhastened by my hand. O guide and aid my dear son, if he still be alive! Adieu, my friend!

[He falls forward.]

Edgar: Adieu, sir, I have gone. I fear that perhaps imagination may, after all, be strong enough to deprive a man of even life itself, especially when life is ready to be surrendered. If I had really placed him where he thinks I have, all power to think would, by this time, have been gone. I wonder if he is still living. Halloa, sir! You, friend. Can you hear me speak, sir? He might look like this were he really dead, but his consciousness is returning. Who are you, sir?

Gloucester: Leave me to die in peace!

Edgar: You must be made of the very lightest of all light things. If you had weighed more than down, you would have been dashed to pieces on falling from such a height! Yet you actually have weight. You are not injured; you can speak and draw your breath. It is most marvellous that you are not dead. Ten tall masts end to end would not reach the height from which you have fallen. Let me hear your voice once more.

Gloucester: Have I really fallen or am I mistaken?

Edgar: Yes, from the terrible height of this chalk cliff. Look up to the top. We cannot hear the notes of the shrill-throated lark that sings over the summit. See for yourself.

Gloucester: Alas! I have no power to see anything, having lost my eyes. O, can misery be denied even the solace of putting an end to its sorrows by death? There was consolation in the thought that a way could still be found to deceive the oppressor and thwart his evil and cruelty.

Edgar: Let me take your arms. Try to stand up. There; how do you feel? What of your legs? Can you stand?

Gloucester: Better than I wish!

Edgar: It is a most marvellous thing! What creature was it that left you on the summit of the rock?

Gloucester: An unhappy, wandering beggar.

76

Edgar: As I looked upon him from here, his eyes appeared huge and round as the moon. He seemed to have numberless noses and protruding horns upon his head, curled and curved in ridges, like the ripples on the water. It must have been an evil spirit. Therefore, you, most fortunate old man, have been saved by the special intervention of heaven, which finds its opportunities in man's extremity of need.

Gloucester: I think that must be so, for the creature who led me often cried out, "The fiend, the fiend." But I still imagined that it was a human being, plagued by an evil spirit. From this time forward, I will patiently endure all my woes, until sorrow itself can do no more, but must surely cease.

Edgar: Try to be resigned and let your mind forget its sorrows. But who is this approaching?

> *[Enter Lear, fantastically dressed with wild flowers.]*
Surely sober sense would never dress its master in this fashion!

Lear: No one can punish me for coining, for I am myself the sovereign.

Edgar: O heartbreaking spectacle!

Lear: Art must yield to nature there. Here is your enlistment money, fellow. There is a man who knows no better than a crow-scarer how to use a bow and arrows; draw me a cloth-yard shaft. See, see, a mouse. Quiet, quiet; here is a piece of toasted cheese. I throw down my gage of battle and will prove my words even against a giant. Advance, halberds! O, well shot! In the center, in the center! Here! Give the password.

Edgar: Sweet marjoram.

Lear: Pass!

Gloucester: I recognize those tones!

Lear: Ha! there is my daughter, with a white beard! They flattered me like a dog and told me I had the wisdom of age while I still owned to the folly of youth. They agreed with everything I said. To say "Yes" and "No," as well, could not possibly be truth. When the rain drenched me and the wind set me shivering, after the thunder rolled on in spite of me, then I found out the liars. The flatterers were exposed! They are deceivers, rogues. They told me I was everything. They were wrong, I was not proof against the chills and fever.

Gloucester: I recognize the tones of that voice. It is the king, is it not?

Lear: Yes, a king to the last drop of blood! Look how my subjects shrink back before my glance! What is your petition, good sir? I give that man a free pardon. Good chemist, let me have some scent to refresh my memory. Here is payment for it.

Gloucester: Let me raise that hand to my lips.

Lear: Wait until I rub it. It smells of death!

Gloucester: O what destruction of a noble work! What ruinous loss of greatness! Even so shall this mighty universe fall to decay. Do you remember me?

Lear: I know your eyes perfectly well. Is it at me you are screwing them up? Nay, the god of love is blind, but he may do what he will for me. I will love no one. Read this challenge, sir. Only notice the writing!

Gloucester: I could not see a single letter, even if they all shone as bright as the sun.

Edgar: I would not believe this when I heard it. My heart aches to find that it is true.

Lear: Read it.

Gloucester: How? With empty eye-sockets?

Lear: Oh! is that how it is? Blind and poor? Both eyes and pockets are in a bad case, though one is heavy and the other light. Yet you see how we fare in this world.

Gloucester: I see it by my own experience.

Lear: What, are you no wiser than that? A man does not need eyes to see how the world goes. You need only listen and you will hear. Hear how yonder judge reproves that poor silly thief? Let me whisper! Let their positions be changed, and then see which is the judge and which the robber! You have seen a farmer's dog bark at a beggar?

Gloucester: Aye, my lord.

Lear: And seen the human being flee before the animal? There you may see a good representation of power and place. Set even a cur in a position of authority, and he will command obedience. A cheat is hanged, though probably the man who pronounces his sentence is himself a usurer. The smallest faults can be plainly seen in one clothed in rags. Let a man but be clothed in rich garments, and not an imperfection will be perceived. Let vice simply be gilded with wealth, and justice is powerless to reach it. But it is far otherwise if vice be accompanied by poverty. I tell you, none are guilty, none. I'll warrant them. Believe me, good sir, when I tell you this, I, who have authority over you all. Go, get glass eyes for yourself and then pretend, like a contemptible politician, that you see clearly the things which you do not see at all. Now, now, now, now. Pull off my boots. Harder, harder! There!

Edgar: What an intermingling of sense and nonsense, of wisdom and foolishness!

Lear: Here are my eyes, if you wish to weep for my sorrows. I remember you. You are the Earl of Gloucester. We must resign ourselves to our fate. We come into the world weeping. At our very first breath, you know, we weep and wail. I will give you a sermon; listen to me!

Gloucester: Alas! alas!

Lear: At the moment of our birth, we weep that we have been brought on this scene where we have to associate with so many fools. This is a well-shaped hat! It would be a clever idea to have a regiment of horses shod with felt. I will do it, for then we could steal noiselessly up to our enemies, my daughters' husbands, and, when I had taken them by surprise, I would slay them, slay them! Slay, slay, slay!

[Enter a gentleman, with attendants.]

Gentleman: We have found him at last. Hold him now. Sir, your beloved daughter . . .

Lear: Am I captured? Without hope of rescue? What a trick fortune has played upon me! I beg you, treat me kindly, and my ransom shall be paid. Bring a doctor to see me, for my head is sorely wounded.

Gentleman: We will let you have whatever you wish, sir.

Lear: Am I to have no seconds? Must I fight alone? Why, it is enough to make a man melt and flush the water out of his eyes like showers that water the dusty lanes in autumn.

I will meet my death as valiantly and joyfully as a self-satisfied bridegroom. Come, I will be glad. See you, sirs, I am a king. Understand me, good people!

Gentleman: You are, sir, a most kingly ruler and you may command us.

Lear: Then there's life in it, and, if you get it, you shall run for it. So off we go!

[Exit running. Attendants follow.]

Gentleman: A pathetic sight! It would be a sad enough spectacle even if it were the most forlorn creature who thus suffered. In a monarch, the tragedy is beyond words! One child is left to you, poor king, who will make amends for the misery the other two have caused.

Edgar: Save you, good sir!

Gentleman: God prosper you, friend. What do you wish?

Edgar: Have you heard it said that a battle is soon to take place?

Gentleman: Certainly. It is common knowledge. Everyone who can hear at all has heard that.

Edgar: Pardon me, I beg, but be kind enough to tell me whether the opposing forces are near at hand.

Gentleman: Quite near and marching rapidly. Every moment it is expected that the main body will come in sight.

Edgar: I only wished to know that, sir. Many thanks.

Gentleman: The queen's forces are advancing to meet the enemy, although she herself has remained behind for important reasons.

Edgar: Many thanks, sir.

[Exit gentleman.]

Gloucester: Kind and merciful heaven, end my life when you will. Preserve me from yielding again to the temptation of taking my own life before the hour you have decreed.

Edgar: A right and proper prayer, my aged friend.

Gloucester: Who may you be, sir?

Edgar: A man, lonely and destitute, who has learned that it is useless to rebel against fate and who also, from experiencing most moving griefs of his own, has a heart full of sympathy and compassion for the woes of others. Let me take your hand, and I will guide you to some suitable place.

Gloucester: I am most grateful. May the gods shower blessings upon you again and again!

[Enter Oswald.]

Oswald: A published outlaw, with a price upon his head! How fortunate! That blind old head was born to be the means of making me rich! Miserable, treacherous old man, make your peace with heaven quickly, for the weapon that is to take your life is already drawn.

Gloucester: Now, friend, show the power of that kindly arm!

[Edgar interposes.]

Oswald: Bold fellow, how dare you aid one who has been proclaimed as a rebel and outlaw? Begone, in case you have to share the punishment waiting for him. Take your hand from his arm!

Edgar: That I shall not do so, sir, unless you give me a better reason.

Oswald: Villain, take your hand away, or I will slay you.

Edgar: Go your own way, sir, and let poor people go theirs. If I could have been frightened out of my life by bold words, I should have been dead a couple of weeks ago. Nay, nay, keep off. Do not touch the old man, I warn you, or I shall see whether your head or my club will break soonest, I tell you plainly.

Oswald: Away, vile peasant!

[They fight.]

Edgar: My club shall find your head, sir. Come, fight! I care nothing for your nice fencing!

[Oswald falls.]

Oswald: You have killed me, scoundrel! Knave, take my purse and, if you hope to prosper, see that I am buried. Take the papers which I am carrying and look for Edmund, Earl of Gloucester, among the British troops. When you have found him, deliver the papers safely into his hands. O death, death, you come too soon!

[Dies.]

Edgar: I recognize him: a useful knave, who was ready to go to any lengths of wickedness in obedience to his mistress' wishes.

Gloucester: Have you really killed him?

Edgar: Good old man, be seated here and rest. I will examine his pockets. The paper that he mentioned may be very useful to me. Yes, I have killed him, and my only regret is that it fell to my lot to be his executioner. Now, I will see what this contains. By your leave, kind seal! And let no one say I am discourteous in thus opening it, or guilty of a dishonorable act. We would open our foes' very bosoms, if we could, to find out their thoughts and plans; how much more their letters!

[Reads.] Remember the vows we have sworn to each other. You will have a hundred chances to be rid of him, if you desire the opportunity. Favorable moments will be

81

plentiful. If he comes back victorious, it will seem no gain to me. We shall be no nearer our desires, for I shall still be bound to him. Set me free, and occupy his position for your pains.

Your affectionate servant — I wish I could say your loving wife — *Goneril.*

O, who can set bounds to a woman's will, or say how far her passion reaches! Here is a vile plan to bring about the death of the noble duke and to set my brother, Edmund, in his place. I will cover you up in the earth here, you unholy messenger of wickedness. When the proper time arrives, I shall show this cruel letter to the duke, whose death has been so wickedly plotted, and startle him with its contents. It is a good thing for him that I can both bring tidings of your death, vile creature, and warn him of the errand you travelled on.

Gloucester: The king has lost his reason. But my bodily strength is so unbending, my faculties so unyielding, that my sorrows have not yet conquered me, or overwhelmed my brain. Consequently, I am still fully conscious of my great and keen sufferings. It were better that I were mad, for then my mind could not dwell on its sorrows, for grief which does not recognize itself as such is not felt.

[Drum afar off.]

Edgar: Come, let me lead you. I think I hear drums in the distance. Come, old man, and I will commit you to the charge of a friend.

[Exeunt.]

ACT IV • SCENE 7

[A tent in the French camp.]
[Lear on a bed asleep, soft music playing.
Gentleman and others attending.]
[Enter Cordelia, Kent and doctor.]

Cordelia: O my kind friend, what can I do in return for all your kindness? How can I repay you? Anything I may do will fall short of what you deserve, and my whole life will not be sufficiently long to show all my gratitude.

Kent: I am more than repaid, sweet lady, by your thanks and the knowledge that you understand what I have tried to do. All that I have told you is the bare truth, neither modified nor exaggerated, but exactly as it occurred.

Cordelia: I should like to see you in a dress more befitting your rank. Those garments cannot fail to remind you of the miseries you have endured. Discard them, I urge you.

Kent: Forgive me, sweet lady, but I have firmly resolved not to reveal myself yet. Let me beg you, as a favor, to seem ignorant of my real name until I shall think the time has arrived for you to recognize me openly.

Cordelia: In that case, I agree, my friend. *[To the doctor.]* How is my father?

Doctor: He is still sleeping, lady.

Cordelia: O gracious and pitying heaven, heal his frail body, racked and overstrained by the cruelties he has endured. Restore his unstrung faculties, so altered by his daughters' ungrateful conduct.

Doctor: Do you not think that the king might safely be aroused now? His slumber has lasted for some time.

Cordelia: Good sir, be guided by your own wisdom and do what you judge to be the best. Has the king been clothed afresh?

Gentleman: Yes, my lady. His clothes were changed while he still slept soundly.

Doctor: Remain close at hand, dear lady, while he is aroused, and I have no fear but that he will be calm.

Cordelia: I will do so.

Doctor: Come closer still, I pray. Musicians, play more loudly.

Cordelia: Beloved father! May the touch of my lips be as a healing balm, and this loving caress make amends for the savage injuries that my sisters inflicted on your honored form!

Kent: Sweet and beloved lady!

Cordelia: Surely these gray hairs might have claimed compassion from them, even had you not been their own parent! This reverend face should never have been exposed to the rude blows of the tempest, or been compelled to brave the awful thunder-bolt and the fierce, keen lightning-flash. And to think, poor lost, forlorn one, that you had to wander through the wild night with only this scanty covering! On that tempestuous night, I could not have refused shelter and warmth even to a dog, though it belonged to my foe and had bitten me, and to think that my poor father was thankful for the shelter of a miserable hut, with foul straw for his bed and poor, lost wretches for company! Alas! It would have been no marvel if both life and reason had given way together. See, he is awaking. Speak to him.

Doctor: It is better that you should do so, madam.

Cordelia: How is your majesty? How do you feel now?

Lear: You are unkind not to let me sleep quietly in my grave! You, I know, are an angel of paradise, but I am fastened to a burning wheel and, when I weep, my tears burn, too.

Cordelia: Do you know who I am, my lord?

Lear: Yes, you are an angel. How long ago did you die?

Cordelia: He wanders yet!

Doctor: Wait a little till he is more fully awake.

Lear: Where have I been? Where am I? Is it bright daylight? O, I am shamefully treated. If I saw any man so wretched as I am, I should die of sorrow for him. I am not sure of anything. I could not say whether these hands are mine, but I will try. Yes, I feel this pin pierce me. I wish I knew anything with certainty, but I am greatly confused!

Cordelia: O my dear father, look at me and bless me! Nay, it is not right that you should kneel to me.

Lear: Do not deceive me, I beg. I am an aged man, eighty years old, in deed and truth, and very simple and foolish. To tell you the truth, I am very much afraid that my mind is wandering. It appears to me that your face ought to be known to me and, also, that I should be acquainted with this man, but I cannot be at all certain. I am entirely unable to remember this place, nor with all my thinking can I account for these clothes I am wearing. Neither can I recall where I passed the night. Pray, do not think me ridiculous, but I verily believe this lady is my child, Cordelia.

Cordelia: She is, she is your child!

Lear: Are they real tears? Yes, in truth! But, lady, do not cry. I will do what you wish quietly. If you intend to take my life by some deadly drink, I am willing to swallow it. I am sure you hate me, for I recollect that my other daughters have injured me much, without any cause. You have great reason to do so.

Cordelia: No, never! I have no reason!

Lear: Is this France?

Kent: It is your own country, my lord.

Lear: Do not mock me.

84

Doctor: All is well, dear lady. You see the violent passion of insanity has gone, but it would be unwise to let him think too much over what is past. Ask him to retire within and do not let him be further disturbed until his mind is more composed.

Cordelia: Will you come in now, my lord?

Lear: I pray you, have patience with me and pardon me and overlook my faults. I am a simple old man.

[Exeunt all but Kent and gentleman.]

Gentleman: Is the news confirmed, sir, of the death of the Duke of Cornwall?

Kent: Yes, it is quite correct.

Gentleman: Who is leading his troops?

Kent: I hear that Edmund, Gloucester's son, is doing so.

Gentleman: Report says that Edgar, whom the old earl exiled, is in Germany, in company with the banished Kent.

Kent: Rumors are many and various. We must be on the alert now. The native forces are advancing rapidly.

Gentleman: The conflict which will decide the matter has every appearance of being a deadly one. Adieu, sir.

[Exit.]

Kent: My end and fate will be decided also, for better or worse, according to the result of today's fight.

[Exit.]

ACT V • SCENE 1

[The British camp near Dover.]
[Enter, with drums and colors, Edmund, Regan, gentlemen and soldiers.]

Edmund: *[To a gentleman.]* Go and find out from the Duke of Albany whether the orders recently given by him still hold good or whether he has since seen any reason to alter his plans. He is most changeable and unsettled and full of dissatisfaction. Find out what he has finally resolved upon and let me know.

[Exit gentleman.]

Regan: Something has certainly happened to Goneril's messenger.

Edmund: I fear so, lady.

Regan: Dear Gloucester, you are aware of my goodwill towards you and of the benefits I will confer upon you. But I wish to know the truth. Tell me whether you really love Goneril.

Edmund: With a most respectful affection.

Regan: But you have not taken the place left vacant by her husband?

Edmund: That is an unworthy thought.

Regan: I fear that you are a much closer friend than you will admit.

Edmund: I swear that I am not, lady.

Regan: Dear Gloucester, do not take her to your heart. I myself detest her.

Edmund: Do not be afraid. But here she comes, with the duke accompanying her!

[Enter, with drum and colors, Albany, Goneril and soldiers.]

Goneril: *[Aside.]* I would rather we were defeated than that Regan should come between Edmund and me!

Albany: Greeting, my dear Regan! The latest news, sir, is that the aged Lear and others who have been driven by harsh treatment are now with Cordelia. I have never been able to show myself bold in an unworthy cause. If I cannot take up a quarrel whole-heartedly, I prefer to avoid the struggle, and, in this case, the fact that the French troops have invaded our country is what concerns us. I take up arms against them, not as the friends of Lear, but as the enemies of our country, which they, with others who have suffered much injustice at our hands, are come to subdue.

Edmund: Your sentiments do you honor, sir.

Regan: Why do you speak of these matters just now?

Goneril: The most pressing need at present is that we should all make common cause against our foes. This is neither the time nor place to bring up private quarrels and side issues.

Albany: Let us take counsel, then, with the most experienced commanders and settle our plans.

Edmund: I shall wait upon your grace shortly at your tent.

Regan: You will accompany us, Goneril?

Goneril: I had rather not.

Regan: I beg you, do so; it is much better that you should.

Goneril: *[Aside.]* Oh! I see what you mean. Very well.

[As they are going out, enter Edgar, disguised.]

Edgar: Listen to me, my lord, for one instant, if you ever condescend to speak to one such as I am.

Albany: I will be with you presently, friends. Now, my good fellow, what have you to say?

[Exeunt all but Albany and Edgar.]

Edgar: Open this and read it before you enter the fight. If you should win, then summon the messenger to appear before you, for notwithstanding my poor appearance, I can furnish proof that the information contained in that letter is true and will provide a challenger to take up the quarrel. Should you be defeated, or slain in the battle, of course, that ends your interest in the events of this life, and plots against you cease to have any object. The gods befriend you!

Albany: Wait until I see what this news is.

Edgar: I must not do so, but let the trumpet summon me when I am required and you shall see me then.

Albany: Adieu, then, and I will read the letter.

[Exit Edgar.]
[Re-enter Edmund.]

Edmund: Our forces must be marshalled at once. The opposing army is in sight. This is the nearest calculation of their numbers and power that could be discovered by careful scouting. Now we must move with all speed.

Albany: We will be ready for the event.

[Exit.]

Edmund: I have vowed affection to both the old king's daughters, and each one suspects her sister, even as those who have once been bitten never again trust a snake.

Which shall it be? Goneril? Regan? Or neither of them? As long as either lives, I can have no peace with the other. If I marry Regan, whose husband is dead, Goneril will be mad with jealousy. As long as Goneril's husband lives, I shall have difficulty in furthering my plans. We will make use of him until this fighting is over and, after that, leave it to the one who wishes for his absence to invent some plan to bring about his death. Let this fight be once over, and the old king and his youngest daughter at our mercy, and Albany shall not have the chance to show them the kindness he intends. It remains for me now to defend my position, not to waste time in deliberating.

[Exit.]

ACT V • SCENE 2

[A field between the two armies.]
[Alarum within. Enter, with drum and colors, Lear, Cordelia and soldiers, over the stage, and exeunt.]
[Enter Edgar and Gloucester.]

Edgar: Good old man, let this tree shelter you for awhile. Rest here and pray for the success of the righteous cause. If ever I come back in safety, I shall give you news that will gladden your heart.

Gloucester: Heaven be good to you, friend!

[Exit Edgar.]
[Alarum and retreat within. Re-enter Edgar.]

Edgar: Good father, we must fly! Let me lead you; come! Lear's foes have triumphed, and he is taken prisoner, and Cordelia also. Come, come away!

Gloucester: Not a step farther. This place will do as well as any other to die in.

Edgar: What! Are you unhappy again? Do not give way to sadness. The circumstances of our birth and our death are beyond our control. We must bear patiently the time of death decreed for us, as well as the manner. The only thing that matters is our readiness. Let us go!

Gloucester: You are right, my friend.

[Exeunt.]

ACT V · SCENE 3

[The British camp near Dover.]
[Enter, in conquest, with drum and colors, Edmund, Lear and
Cordelia, prisoners, captain, soldiers etc.]

Edmund: Remove these prisoners, someone, and see that they are well guarded. Their fate lies in the hands of those of higher rank than I, and we must await their decision.

Cordelia: Many innocent and well-intentioned persons, before our day, have suffered heavy misfortune. For my part, I could defy ill-chance and endure injustice, but my heart is heavy for your sake, poor persecuted king and father. Shall we wait and speak to these women, who are my sisters and your daughters?

Lear: No, no! By no means see them! Let us go to our prison together. There we will keep each other company and pass the time as happily as birds in captivity, singing to each other, and, when you beg me to bless you, I will reply by begging of you to pardon me, so we will each make request of the other and gladly grant it. Then we will say our prayers and tell old stories and amuse ourselves with pretty trifles and listen to all the gossip of the court. We will join in it, too, and take an interest in the varying fortunes of courtier and noble and hear who are the favored ones of the moment and who are looked upon with ill-will. Then we will converse of the marvels of the universe, the hidden powers of heaven and the wondrous ways of heaven's dealings with men, as if we could follow all their varying course and see heaven's wisdom in all. Oh, yes! In our close and narrow place of confinement, we shall yet outlive many a court faction and party of exalted ones, who rise and fall with every change of the weather!

Edmund: Remove these prisoners!

Lear: Heaven joyfully accepts such offerings as this, my daughter. At last I have found you! Those who wish to take us away from each other now will have to do it by fire, as foxed are smoked out of their holes. Do not weep. Dry your tears. May they be consumed, body and hide, by disease, before they see us shed tears! Let them die sooner! Let us go away! Let us go!

[Exeunt Lear and Cordelia, guarded.]

Edmund: Officer, come near and listen to me. Take this letter *[giving a paper]* and go after Lear and his daughter to their place of confinement. I have already promoted you, and, if you follow out the instructions contained in this note, you will place yourself on the high road to honor and wealth. Understand that men must do as they are compelled by the necessities of the age and a soft heart is of no use to a soldier. This important task that I have entrusted to you is not a question to be argued about. You must either promise to perform it, or make up your mind to seek some other means of advancement, for you need not look for any further favor from me.

Captain: It shall be performed, sir.

Edmund: Set about it at once, then, and account yourself a fortunate man when it is accomplished. Now notice, I have said it is to be done at once, and exactly as your instructions direct.

Captain: If it lies within the power of a man to do it and does not require the strength of a horse or an ass, it shall be done.

[Exit.]

[Flourish. Enter Albany, Goneril, Regan,
another captain and soldiers.]

Albany: You have shown great courage in today's fight, sir, and have been most fortunate in the result. The prisoners, who were our antagonists in the recent battle, are in your possession. Be good enough to deliver them into my hands, so that they may receive such treatment as they deserve, consistent with the welfare of the state.

Edmund: It seemed best to me, sir, to give orders for the confinement of the aged Lear, for the hearts of the people will be readily turned in his favor, both by his weight of years and his former position as monarch. Thus, we may find that our present followers may turn their weapons against us, on his behalf. For the same reason, I sent Cordelia into imprisonment also. Whenever it pleases you to hold a court for their trial, you have only to summon them before you. Just at the present moment, we are overcome by the fierceness of the recent conflict. Our thoughts are occupied with the losses we have sustained, and, in the trials of the moment, even those who are in the right feel anger against the cause for which they suffer so much. It appears to me that this is no suitable moment in which to raise the question of the treatment of the old king and his daughter.

Albany: Pardon me, sir, but you must not forget that you are my subordinate, not my equal.

Regan: That is for me to decide. If I choose to place him in a position of equality, he is no longer a subordinate. I think it would have been as well had you referred to me before speaking so decidedly. He took my place in rank and in the leadership of the troops and, in that position of authority, may certainly be considered your equal.

Goneril: Calm yourself, sister! He is sufficiently noble in himself and does not need to wait for promotion from you.

Regan: If I choose to advance him, he may equal the noblest in the land!

Goneril: You had better raise him as high as possible by marrying him.

Regan: Many a truth is spoken in jest.

Goneril: Oh, indeed! I don't think, however, that it is likely to be so in this case.

Regan: I could reply to that very fully and convincingly, but at present I am feeling ill. Gloucester, I here deliver into your hands my troops, the captives we have taken and all my wealth. They and I, and all that I possess, are alike yours to do with as you will. Let every one bear witness that I do acknowledge you from henceforth as my ruler and head!

Goneril: And will you marry him?

Albany: Whether she does or does not, it is not for you to decide.

Edmund: Nor for you either, sir!

Albany: There you are mistaken!

Regan: *[To Edmund.]* Bid the drum sound, and I will invest you with my powers before all the army.

Albany: Not so fast! You must first listen to me. I here arrest you, Edmund, as a traitor, and this false woman *[pointing to Goneril]* is also involved in your disgrace. And as to you, good madam, who wish to marry this traitor, I must oppose your claim on my wife's behalf. She is the one who is pledged to him, so that I, her spouse, cannot allow him to wed with you. There is no one left to be your husband but myself. My wife is spoken for!

Goneril: A pretty play!

Albany: You still carry your weapons, sir. If no one comes forth at the sound of the trumpet blast to establish the truth of this accusation against you that you are a proved and hateful traitor, I here challenge you myself, and there is my gage *[throwing down a glove]*. Before I taste food again, I will prove the truth on your body, that of the wickedness of which I have accused you, you stand guilty!

Regan: Oh! I feel ill!

Goneril: *[Aside.]* If you were not, it would be wonderful, after the drink you have swallowed.

Edmund: *[Throwing down a glove.]* There is my acceptance of your challenge, and whoever accuses me of treachery is a villainous liar! I will uphold my integrity and honesty with my sword against him, against you or against anyone else in the world who may venture to take up the challenge.

Albany: Let a herald approach!

Edmund: A herald, ho! Send a herald!

Albany: Do not look for any aid from your troops. They are already, by my orders, disbanded, as they were summoned by my authority.

Regan: I feel much worse; my sickness is increasing.

Albany: Take her into my tent. She is ill.

[Exit Regan, led.]
[Enter a herald.]

Herald, come near. Let the trumpeter blow a blast; then proclaim this aloud.

Captain: Sound trumpet!

[A trumpet sounds.]

Herald: *[Reads.]* "If any person of rank or noble lineage among our troops is prepared to prove that Edmund, called Earl of Gloucester, is guilty of many treacheries, let him come forth when the trumpet shall have sounded three times. The accused Edmund boldly asserts his innocence."

Edmund: Blow!   *[First trumpet.]*

Herald: Again!   *[Second trumpet.]*

Herald: Once more!   *[Third trumpet.]*

[Trumpet answers within.]
[Enter Edgar, at the third sound, armed, with a trumpet before him.]

Albany: Enquire what brings him here and why he answers the challenge of the trumpet-call.

Herald: Declare to us your name and rank and the reason which has led you to come and take up this quarrel!

Edgar: I have no longer a name. The corroding touch of treachery has seized upon it to its ruin. But my rank and lineage are equal to those of the antagonist against whom I have come to strive.

Albany: Whom do you appear against?

Edgar: Who stands for Edmund of Gloucester?

Edmund: Edmund of Gloucester. What have you to say to him?

Edgar: Here is my weapon. Take yours in hand, so that it may strike for the right, if what I say shall wound your honest heart. My rank, my profession and my knightly oath alike give me the right thus to declare that, in spite of your prowess, your youthful vigor, your courage and high mettle, in spite of the high position you have attained, the victory you have just gained and the brand-new honors now heaped upon you, you are false, treacherous and perjured — false to your own nearest and dearest and false before heaven, an intriguer against this noble lord and, in every part of you, wholly false, perjured and faithless! If you deny it, I intend to prove upon your heart, which my words are meant to reach, that you utter a lie, and, to that end, all my powers of mind and body shall be directed.

Edmund: If I were prudent, I should make you reveal yourself, but I accept the warrant of your soldierly appearance and gentlemanly speech, and though, if I were disposed to be scrupulously exact according to the rules of combats such as this, I might, with safety, refuse to meet you, I scorn to do so. I fling your accusations back in your teeth and return to you your name of "liar." With my sword's point, I will cleave a way for them to your heart, where they shall be driven home! Sound the onset!

[Alarums. They fight. Edmund falls.]

Albany: Stop! Do not take his life yet.

Goneril: O Edmund! This has been an arranged plot. By the rules of knighthood, you could have refused to fight a foe who would not reveal himself. You have been deceived and trapped, not conquered fairly!

Albany: Say no more, woman, or I shall prevent you with a sight of this letter! Now, sir, you unspeakably vile wretch, look at the written evidence of your own wickedness. No, madam, you shall not tear it; I see that you recognize it.

[Gives the letter to Edmund.]

Goneril: And what matter if I know it? It is I who rule, not you! No one can bring me to trial for what I do.

Albany: Oh! most terrible! You do know it, then?

Goneril: I will not be questioned about it.

[Exit.]

Albany: Let someone follow her and restrain her. She is almost beside herself.

Edmund: I confess. I am guilty of all that I have been accused of, and of worse still. Time will soon reveal what I have done. It is ended, and my life also. But who are you, my adversary, who have thus chanced to be the conqueror? I will not resent it if you are nobly born.

Edgar: Let us both give and take forgiveness. I am as nobly born as yourself, Edmund. If my birth is even better, then so much the greater is your fault. I am your brother, Edgar. Heaven's retribution is exact. The sins we take delight in are the very means by which we are undone. The hidden misdeeds of my father lost him his sight.

Edmund: That is the truth. My evils have returned upon my own head, and here I lie!

Albany: Let me clasp you to my heart! I seemed to see the promise of nobility in your every movement. May my bosom burst with grief, if ever I was an enemy of either the aged earl or yourself!

Edgar: I was assured of that, noble lord.

Albany: Where were you concealed? And how did you know of the misfortunes that had befallen your father?

Edgar: I became acquainted with them by fortunately being able to relieve them. I will tell your grace as shortly as I can, and I should be thankful if my heart would break when the tale is over. When I found myself under the instant necessity of escaping from those who were searching for me, according to the cruel proclamation which outlawed me, I learnt to disguise myself and put on the wretched rags and appearance of a maniac, to appear such a forlorn and miserable creature that even the brute beasts scorned me. How strange that mere life should be so dear to us that we should passionately cling to it and should be willing to endure, day after day, pangs equal to those of death in order to retain our hold on life, rather than suffer death once and for all.

While I wore this diguise, I found my father wandering in darkness, his face still bleeding from his cruel injuries, those precious possessions, his eyes, having been newly torn from their sockets. From that time, I took him into my charge, found food for him and rescued him from the state of hopelessness into which he had fallen and which had led him to attempt to take his life. I never told him who I was until within the last hour, when I came armed to the combat. For that I now blame myself much, but then I asked his fatherly benediction, as I could not know whether I should have the good fortune to vanquish my opponent, though I hoped to return in safety to him. I begged him to bless me and told him of all my wanderings from the beginning, but his heart, already weakened by suffering, could bear no more. The mingled emotions of gladness and sorrow overcame him, and his heart broke with excess of joy.

Edmund: I am greatly affected by what you have said. Perhaps it may be of some benefit to me. But continue; you appear to have further news for us.

Albany: If you have more to tell and it be any worse tidings than this, let it remain unsaid. I am melted to tears by what you have already related.

Edgar: One would have thought that here grief had reached its limit. To enlarge upon another such occurrence would be to go beyond all extremes. Yet such another comes. While I was crying out in grief, a man approached me, who had seen me in my wretched rags. He had then avoided me with loathing, but now, on discovering that it was I, Gloucester's son, who had borne that misery, he threw his arms around my neck and wept aloud, as though his grief would tear the skies. Then he embraced my father's dead body and commenced to relate a most heart-rending story of what had befallen the aged king and himself. As he proceeded, his sorrow proved too strong for him. He could not finish the tale. His heart was breaking. Then I heard the first two trumpet-calls and was forced to leave him there, unconscious.

Albany: And who was the man?

Edgar: The Earl of Kent, my lord: Kent, who had been sentenced to exile by the king and who had disguised himself and, in the capacity of a servant who befriended the man who had treated him so ill, following him and rendering him the most menial services with faithful loyalty.

[Enter a gentleman with a bloody knife.]

Gentleman: Oh! help, help! Some assistance!

Edgar: Assistance for what?

Albany: What is it?

Edgar: Why is that knife stained with blood?

Gentleman: It is still warm from the heart of — oh! she is slain!

Albany: Who? Tell us quickly!

Gentleman: Your wife, your wife, my lord! She confessed to having poisoned her sister and then slew herself.

Edmund: I had made vows to each of them. Now we three are all joined by death!

Edgar: Here is the Earl of Kent approaching.

Albany: Let both the bodies be brought here, whether living or not. We cannot feel sorrow on their account, though the swiftness with which the gods have punished their crimes fills our minds with awe.

[Exit gentleman.]
[Enter Kent.]

Is this the faithful Kent, of whom you spoke? Sir, in courtesy we should pay you our thanks and good wishes, were this a fitting moment.

Kent: I have come to take a last farewell of my master and sovereign. I thought to find him here.

Albany: How could we forget so important a matter! Where is he, Edmund? And where is his daughter? Do you see this spectacle, Kent?

[The bodies of Goneril and Regan are brought in.]

Kent: Alas! What has brought them to this?

Edmund: Edmund, in spite of all, had still the power to inspire affection! One took the other's life for love of me and then took her own.

Albany: Yes, thus it was. Cover their faces.

Edmund: My breath is almost gone, but I will yet do one good deed before it fails, unused though I am to the doing of a good action. Let someone go swiftly to the castle and waste no time, for I have sent an order to put the king and his daughter to death. Quick! Do not be too late!

Albany: Oh, hurry! hurry!

Edgar: Who has your order, sir? Give me a sign that I come from you and that their lives are to be spared.

Edmund: That is well remembered! Here is my sword. Take it to the commanding officer.

Albany: Hurry! Run with all speed!

[Exit Edgar.]

Edmund: The order to the captain was sent from Goneril and myself. Cordelia was to be hanged in the castle, but it was to appear as though she had taken her own life in extremity of despair.

Albany: Heaven be her aid! Let this man be carried away from here.

[Edmund is borne off.]
[Re-enter Lear, with Cordelia, dead in his arms,
Edgar, captain and others following.]

Lear: Cry! Cry aloud! Howl, weep and howl! Oh! you are hard-hearted! Had I your voices, I would cleave the very heavens with my lamentations, looking on this sad sight. Her spirit has fled! She has departed forever! I know the look of death too well to doubt. She is lifeless clay! But let us see if her breath will cloud a mirror, for then she is not dead!

Kent: This is surely the prophesied end of all things!

Edgar: Or a shadow of that awful day!

Albany: Let it come and all things now cease!

Lear: She is not dead. This feather moves. She is not dead! Oh! if that prove true, the blessed truth will overpay me for all my miseries.

Kent: *[Kneeling.]* Dear master!

Lear: Begone, I pray you!

Edgar: It is your faithful friend, the good Earl of Kent.

Lear: Curses on you all! Treacherous assassins! She might have been saved, and now I have lost her forever! Cordelia, my child, my daughter, do not leave me yet! Ah! What did you say? Her tones were always so soft and sweet, a most attractive trait in a woman! I slew the villain that took your sweet life!

Captain: He did indeed, sirs.

Lear: It is true, sirrah, is it not! There was once a time when I could have driven them all before me at the sword's point. I am an aged man now, worn out by my sorrows. Who are you, sir? To speak plainly, I do not see so well now.

Kent: Here is one who has endured the farthest extremes of fortune's good and ill, no matter who the other may be, if there be more than one.

Lear: Here is a sad spectacle! I think you are the Earl of Kent, are you not?

Kent: I am the very man, your faithful servant. Where is Caius, who used to follow you?

Lear: Oh, he's a capital fellow. He will certainly lose no time in fighting. Why, he died long enough ago for his body to be completely decayed by now.

Kent: No, my dear master, I am Caius, who served you—

Lear: I will look into it at once.

Kent: From the very beginning of your misfortunes and never left you . . .

Lear: I am glad to see you.

Kent: I, and no other, it was. And now all is gloom and sadness. Goneril and Regan, in despair, have taken their own lives.

Lear: Yes, I think they have.

Albany: His mind is wandering again. It is of no use trying to make him understand who we are.

Edgar: Useless indeed!

[Enter a captain.]

Captain: Edmund is dead, sir.

Albany: That is of very little importance. My lords and worthy friends, hear my intentions. I mean to take every possible means to restore and amend the fortunes of this unfortunate country. On my part, I forgo my authority in favor of the aged king as long as he shall live. *[To Kent and Edgar.]* You, sirs, take up your rightful inheritance and place, and such rewards as your faithfulness and loyalty have richly deserved shall be added thereto. Our friends shall find their goodness freely repaid, and our enemies receive the treatment which they merit. Oh! look! See the poor king!

Lear: And my sweet innocent is dead, dead, dead! And such vile creatures as dogs and rats still live, and you are dead! You are gone forever! You will never return to me! Never, never again! Pray, sir, loosen this for me. I thank you. Do you see her? Look at her! See, her lips! See!

[Dies.]

Edgar: He has fainted! My king! My master!

Kent: Oh! Will my heart not break!

Edgar: Look up, sir.

Kent: Trouble not his spirit. Let him go in peace. Only an enemy would be so cruel as to wish him to live any longer in this world of sorrow.

Edgar: He is dead now.

Kent: It is marvellous that his sufferings did not kill him sooner. His life seemed to be prolonged beyond all right.

Albany: Let them be carried away. These many griefs claim our first attention. *[To Kent and Edgar.]* You two beloved friends, dear to my heart, help to govern this cruelly injured country and maintain its almost wrecked position.

Kent: I shall soon be far from here, my lord. I must follow my dear master.

Albany: We must do as we are compelled by these sorrowful events, and our speech bears witness to the grief of our hearts. Those who have lived longest have had the most to endure. We of the younger generation will never experience the like, nor could we endure it so bravely.

[Exeunt, with a dead march.]

NOTES

NOTES

NOTES

NOTES

NOTES

NOTES

NOTES

NOTES

NOTES